Cambridge El

Elements in Religion and Monotheism
edited by
Paul K. Moser
Loyola University Chicago
Chad Meister
*Affiliate Scholar, Ansari Institute for Global Engagement with Religion,
University of Notre Dame*

THE ABRAHAMIC VERNACULAR

Rebecca Scharbach Wollenberg
University of Michigan

Shaftesbury Road, Cambridge CB2 8EA, United Kingdom

One Liberty Plaza, 20th Floor, New York, NY 10006, USA

477 Williamstown Road, Port Melbourne, VIC 3207, Australia

314–321, 3rd Floor, Plot 3, Splendor Forum, Jasola District Centre,
New Delhi – 110025, India

103 Penang Road, #05–06/07, Visioncrest Commercial, Singapore 238467

Cambridge University Press is part of Cambridge University Press & Assessment,
a department of the University of Cambridge.

We share the University's mission to contribute to society through the pursuit of
education, learning and research at the highest international levels of excellence.

www.cambridge.org
Information on this title: www.cambridge.org/9781009517171

DOI: 10.1017/9781009286787

© Rebecca Scharbach Wollenberg 2024

This publication is in copyright. Subject to statutory exception and to the provisions
of relevant collective licensing agreements, no reproduction of any part may take
place without the written permission of Cambridge University Press & Assessment.

When citing this work, please include a reference to the DOI 10.1017/9781009286787

First published 2024

A catalogue record for this publication is available from the British Library.

ISBN 978-1-009-51717-1 Hardback
ISBN 978-1-009-28675-6 Paperback
ISSN 2631-3014 (online)
ISSN 2631-3006 (print)

Cambridge University Press & Assessment has no responsibility for the persistence
or accuracy of URLs for external or third-party internet websites referred to in this
publication and does not guarantee that any content on such websites is, or will
remain, accurate or appropriate.

The Abrahamic Vernacular

Elements in Religion and Monotheism

DOI: 10.1017/9781009286787
First published online: April 2024

Rebecca Scharbach Wollenberg
University of Michigan

Author for correspondence: Rebecca Scharbach Wollenberg, rwollenb@ umich.edu

Abstract: Contemporary thought typically places a strong emphasis on the exclusive and competitive nature of Abrahamic monotheisms. This instinct is certainly borne out by the histories of religious wars, theological polemic, and social exclusion involving Jews, Christians, and Muslims. But there is also another side to the Abrahamic coin. Even in the midst of communal rivalry, Jews, Christians, and Muslim practitioners have frequently turned to each other to think through religious concepts, elucidate sacred history, and enrich their ritual practices. Scholarship often describes these interactions between the Abrahamic monotheisms using metaphors of exchange between individuals – as if one tradition might borrow a theological idea from another in the same way that a neighbor might borrow a recipe. This Element proposes that there are deeper forms of entanglement at work in these historical moments.

Keywords: Abrahamic, Jewish–Christian relations, Jewish–Muslim relations, vernacular religion, ecumenism

ISBNs: 9781009517171 (HB), 9781009286756 (PB), 9781009286787 (OC)
ISSNs: 2631-3014 (online), 2631-3006 (print)

Contents

1 How This Element Works

1.1 Abrahamic

Before we begin the essay proper, we should briefly explore some of the presuppositions that undergird this Element. Let us begin by unpacking the title. The word "Abrahamic" has become a loaded term in the current moment. In popular parlance, the term Abrahamic religions is often used to emphasize the commonalities between Judaism, Christianity, and Islam for the purposes of interfaith work and community building. But in scholarly circles, the designation Abrahamic is frequently maligned for the way in which it evokes a shared mythic ancestor to create an *illusion* of commonality grounded in a theological or essentialist approach to the study of religion. (The reader can learn more about these concerns below in Section 2.2). This Element acknowledges that Judaism, Christianity, and Islam are not tied together by a historical figure of Abraham – or any other essential theological continuity. Yet we will use the term "Abrahamic" to capture how not only Abraham but also *all* of the scriptural figures shared between these three traditions have served to invite continual imaginative engagement between practitioners of Judaism, Christianity, and Islam as they sought (sometimes competitively and sometimes collaboratively) to cultivate scriptural and religious landscapes that exceeded the boundaries of their particular written revelations. In other words, the term Abrahamic is adopted in this Element to conjure the many ways in which Judaism, Christianity, and Islam have *become* similar over the centuries because they evolved facing each other over shared scriptural tropes.

1.2 Vernacular

Now to the second word in the title. This Element focuses on "vernacular" religion in the sense of "religion as it is lived: as human beings encounter, understand, interpret, and practice it" (Primiano 1995, 44). (The reader can learn more about the category of vernacular religion below in Section 4.2). This essay argues that the three Abrahamic traditions have become subtly inter-twined by their histories of shared lived religion in different times and places. Jewish, Christian, and Muslim practitioners living in close quarters have often participated in overlapping forms of vernacular local religion, so that the conceptions and practices of each community co-evolved in a common cultural religious landscape infused with shared presuppositions about categories such as revelation, scripture, and the divine. This is, of course, true of many different kinds of religious practitioners living in close proximity. But this Element argues that the dynamic has been particularly strong among practitioners of the Abrahamic traditions because they also share a scriptural vernacular. Which is to say, the vernacular religious traditions fostered by practitioners of Judaism, Christianity, and Islam are often constructed around common scriptural figures and narratives. Like speakers of distinctive dialects of the same language, local practitioners rooted in different Abrahamic traditions have inflected this shared scriptural vernacular in distinct (and even competing) ways. Yet many of these local religious dialects were ultimately reabsorbed into the broader traditions of Judaism, Christianity, or Islam. As a result, this Element argues, an ever-changing kaleidoscope of vernacular Abrahamic entwinements has left indelible marks of religious common sense on these three traditions.

1.3 Timeline, Geographic Scope, and Structure

This Element draws examples from nearly two thousand years of religious history and analyzes Abrahamic vernaculars that emerged in far flung geographical locations from Iraq to northern Europe. These diverse examples are then arranged not by historical chronology or geographic region but by theme. In any given section, the reader will thus encounter illustrations of a particular phenomenon or pattern from many different historical contexts – sometimes separated by as many as a dozen centuries or thousands of miles. This wide-ranging thematic structure was chosen to counteract a tendency we see in many works on Jewish, Christian, and Muslim relations in which a particular century in a particular geographic region is hailed as a golden age of intercommunal harmony, while all other historical contexts are treated as times of natural strife between competing traditions. This Element seeks to demonstrate that certain recurring patterns in intercommunal relations have drawn practitioners of Judaism, Christianity, and Islam into shared religious vernaculars in many different times and places. In other words, this Element is structured to demonstrate that the existence of a shared Abrahamic Vernacular has been a fundamental and recurring facet of Jewish, Christian, and Muslim relations throughout many centuries and geographic regions.

2 What Is an Abrahamic Monotheism?

2.1 The Question

What is an Abrahamic monotheism? Or to pose a more radical version of this question: Is there such a thing as Abrahamic monotheism? In the past decade, we have arrived at a strange impasse in the collective study of Judaism(s), Christianit(ies), and Islam(s). We live in a moment when many scholars of religion insist that the historical movements identified with Judaism, Christianity, and Islam cannot be grouped together into any sort of meaningful analytic category. At the same time, scholars of religion are producing more comparative work than ever on the overlaps and intersections between local iterations of Judaism, Christianity, and Islam in various historical periods. As a field, it sometimes seems that we are frantically studying a phenomenon that we claim does not exist.

In the past fifty years, researchers have proposed a succession of models to explain the perceived resemblance or relationship between the so-called Abrahamic traditions. But each new model has ultimately failed to account for at least one vital facet of a complex pattern. As a result, we have reached a point where many scholars insist that no satisfactory analytic category has been discovered because there is none. This Element proposes, in contrast, that we have not been able to produce a satisfactory account of Abrahamic monotheism as a category because we have been approaching the problem backward.

This Element argues that the phenomenon we perceive as Abrahamic monotheism has been produced by a relational constellation. We have been right to recognize a family resemblance between these traditions. But we have been searching for the source of that commonality in the wrong places. It is not structural similarities or theological affinities – or even shared origins – that have bound the Abrahamic monotheisms together into a perceptible category. Rather, it is the very existence of ongoing relational interactions that have ultimately bestowed common character traits on these three traditions.

In their centuries of rivalry over a shared imaginative space, Judaism, Christianity, and Islam evolved facing each other. As a result of this historical orientation toward rival traditions and their claims, practitioners of Judaism, Christianity, and Islam have frequently developed shared local languages of religious imagination that led practitioners to develop overlapping (if sometimes competing) concepts and rituals. *The Abrahamic Vernacular* argues that this shifting kaleidoscope of different historical entanglements has left enduring traces of resemblance on these three traditions – and it is those residual commonalities that generate the category of Abrahamic monotheisms.

2.2 The History of a Category

There was a time when scholars simply referred to Judaism, Christianity, and Islam as the three monotheisms – as if these were the only monotheisms that the human experience had ever produced (Stroumsa 2021).[1] This language certainly reproduces the revolutionary claims made by many historical practitioners of these traditions. But it does not fully reflect the complicated

---

[1] In order to make this Element a more accessible gateway to the topic, I have tried as much as possible to limit my citations of scholarly literature to a very small selection of easily available works in English. I have tried to select examples that contain a rich bibliography of their own – in hopes that readers will be able to pursue for themselves any avenue of inquiry that interests them.

historical realities of Jewish, Christian, and Muslim conceptions of the super-natural, which have often strayed beyond the boundaries of the strictest defin-itions of monotheism (Ali 2010; Fredriksen 2022; MacDonald 2012; Schaefer 2020). More importantly, perhaps, this construction does not recognize the forms of monotheism that other religious traditions have embraced (Flood 2020; Harvey 2019; Mitchell and Van Nuffelen 2010).

When scholars realized that Judaism, Christianity, and Islam could not be differentiated from other religious traditions by their monotheism, many researchers sought to identify other kinds of structural similarities that distin-guished these three traditions as a unique formula of religious expression. These scholars acknowledged that a variety of Greco-Roman and Eastern traditions have included forms of metaphysical monotheism, which posits an eternal divinity that sustains creation. But they maintained that only Judaism, Christianity, and Islam claim that this creator God has revealed his will directly to specific human communities and demanded particular forms of action from these human servants – a religious structure that has been designated by the varied terminologies, including ethical monotheism, prophetic monotheism, revelatory monotheism, and elective monotheism (Jaffee 2001). The types of truth claims made by these elective monotheisms, in turn, were thought to produce certain common categories of religious thought and practice, such as written scripture, revealed tradition, and petitionary prayer (Corrigan et al. 1998). While practitioners of Judaism, Christianity, and Islam have obviously developed each of these categories very differently, proponents of this school of thought argued that the three Abrahamic traditions were nevertheless united by unique structures of religious life.

Critics of this phenomenological school objected that an abstracted vision of a pan-Abrahamic monotheism suppresses the uniqueness of each tradition by creating "a new religion that both encompasses these three and supersedes them" (Levenson 2012, 205). Researchers pointed out that the analogous concept of Judeo-Christian monotheism has long been acknowledged to use claims of a common tradition to overwrite and obscure Jewish difference – remaking diverse and variegated religious histories in the image of Protestant Christianity (Cohen 1969). In the same way, the urge to identify a single Abrahamic concept of revelation, prayer, or providence can serve to eclipse the particularities of Jewish, Christian, and Muslim approaches to common issues (Bakhos 2019, 8).

As definitional categories proved increasingly untenable, some researchers moved to uncover a history of shared origins to explain the aura of commonality within difference that continues to rest on the three Abrahamic traditions. Countless studies have sought to document the possibilities of common origins and identify the exact moments of divergence between these three traditions. When did Judaism and Christianity part ways? Does Islam have Jewish and Christian origins? Where did the various practices and beliefs of the Abrahamic monotheisms originate and how were they disseminated and developed differently in these three traditions? (Stroumsa 2015)

Detractors of the historical approach have argued that this interest in roots is also futile. The imagined origins of a common monotheism promoted by Abraham are beyond our grasp as scholars. Since no neutral historical Abraham can be recovered beyond the oldest limits of sacred history to serve as a check for the three traditions that claim him as founder, we are left instead with what amounts to three distinct Abrahams – three radically incompatible portraits of what it means to be a model servant of the one God (Bakhos 2014). But even if we restrict ourselves to the more modest project of documenting the shared historical origins of these three religious traditions, critics argue that the Abrahamic movements cannot be said to share any substantive common ground when the internecine history that gave birth to Judaism, Christianity, and Islam as distinct traditions has been so often defined by supersessionism, exclusion, and persecution (Hughes 2013).[2] They argue that these traditions were born through difference not commonality.

This is the point at which the discussion has currently stalled. We have reached a moment when many academics are ready to abandon the notion that Judaism, Christianity, and Islam can be conceptualized as related phenomena. Yet what if we approached the current focus on historical conflict as an invitation rather than a closure? Recent theories have dismissed the ongoing history of Jewish, Christian, and Muslim polemic as empty of any true exchange. Because the historical interlocutors were often speaking past each other (debating a particular concept or figure with very different visions of the object in mind), we are tempted to disregard these interactions as meaningless.

Yet the very existence of a continuing history of rivalry, supersessionism, and polemic between Judaism, Christianity, and Islam tells us otherwise. These disputes should not be imagined as a single ongoing (and therefore inevitable) argument. Instead, these moments of polemic represent local phenomena that are continually recreated anew in different times and places. The fact that religious competition repeatedly emerges between these three traditions in different times and places should draw our attention to the fact the imaginary space between these three traditions has consistently been perceived by practitioners as meaningful territory worthy of dispute. The question we need to ask is

---

[2] Although Robert Erlewine argues that is ironically this very tendency to agonism that unites Judaism, Christianity, and Islam in the discursive structure of Abrahamic monotheisms (Erlewine 2010, 10)

why this disputed imaginal space between traditions has been so vital to Jewish, Christian, and Muslim interactions.

2.3 Abrahamic Monotheism as a Relational Constellation

We tend to naturalize the notion that Jews, Christians, and Muslims should tussle over who holds the rights to common intellectual property. But we have already noted that these so-called "Abrahamic" concepts do not have any preexisting substance of their own. There is, in fact, no agreed-upon Abrahamic legacy to dispute. Nor can these recurrent discussions be imagined as the inevitable result of communal proximity and daily friction. In some cases, the interlocutors in these apparent dialogues have no immediate contact at all. The turn toward this shared discursive space can occur even in the absence of any immediate challenge that needs to be addressed or redressed. Instead, that empty space between traditions appears to have some draw, some function, of its own.

What if we explored the possibility that this intersecting space between Judaism, Christianity, and Islam – this central core of the Abrahamic experience – is a *floating signifier* (Levi Strauss 1987, 55–64)? That is, what if this central imaginary is an intellectual space that is named but sufficiently undefined that it can be ascribed different meanings by various interpreters without disrupting the sense that they are speaking of a single object? Or to put it another way, perhaps these three traditions are not bound together by shared mythical and ritual *content* in any substantial sense but are instead united by their shared mythical *signifiers*. In that case, it is less important what each of these three traditions says about Abraham than the formal fact that they all claim to reference the same historical-mythical figure. Similarly, it is not as important how each of these traditions imagines God as it is that these movements all insist that they give ear to a single divine being, the one God who revealed himself to humankind through a historical genealogy of Abraham and his inheritors. While Judaism, Christianity, and Islam have spun these common referents into radically different portraits of revelatory history, they are continuously oriented by them toward a shared discursive space.

Though practically speaking these referents may be empty signifiers, the history of religious conflict between Judaism, Christianity, and Islam has taken place against a backdrop of these shared referents. In the process, the backdrop itself has come to appear natural – even inevitable – to the interlocutors. That is, the very existence of shared referents amidst intercommunal polemic has often produced the impression that there is a neutral sacred history that stands beyond the possibility of dispute and disbelief. While contemporary scholars are quick to point out that Jewish, Christian, and Muslim thinkers paint markedly different (even incompatible) portraits of Moses, for instance, historical practitioners were more likely to conceive of this disconnect as disagreement about a *single* Moses. Through the very process of rivalry over his legacy, Moses's role as a mythical-historical figure within each tradition is naturalized and reinforced by the affirmations of rival traditions. Or to take another example, it is difficult to argue both about the contents of God's prophecy to Moses *and* what it means to receive a prophecy. In any given time and place, a dispute between two Abrahamic communities about the substance of a given prophecy simultaneously had the side effect of naturalizing the shared conceptions of prophecy that undergirded the exchange. After all, the interlocutors in question are doubly primed to speak in a shared religious language by their common historical context and by normative claims that they are speaking about the same phenomena. In such interactions, Abrahamic practitioners thus collectively participate in an imaginary in which both insiders and outsiders alike can be said to acknowledge the veracity of certain premises and histories. In other words, through their very use of shared terminology, the Abrahamic monotheisms acquired companion traditions that have acted not only as competitors but also as partners who obliquely strengthened the worldview of each by affirming an underlying sense of shared reality.

3 Centrifugal and Centripetal Models of Collective Monotheism

When it comes to analyzing historical exchanges between various Abrahamic communities, scholars have tended to reproduce the accounts of these interactions produced by historical practitioners themselves. That is, researchers have traditionally attempted to trace the development of religious differences through the history of Judaism, Christianity, and Islam as if they were biological lineages that spread, branched, and degenerated over time. In doing so, scholars are faithfully reproducing emic motifs widely adopted by the historical practitioners of these three traditions. The history of Jewish–Christian–Muslim polemic is positively littered with familial and biological images of theological family trees, broken branches, and misappropriated prophetic legacies. Many Jewish, Christian, and Muslim practitioners certainly envisioned their own entanglement through a centrifugal paradigm of genealogical growth and separation.

Yet I would argue that the theoretical importance of these emic tropes for our study is precisely the opposite of their own claims. For the most part, the authors of these biological genealogies had as little direct access to the historical origins of the Abrahamic monotheisms as modern academics – and quite possibly less. These portraits of Abrahamic origins must therefore be analyzed as testaments to the religious conceptions of their own time and place. As such, these accounts represent a fascinating window onto an ongoing relational constellation in which Jewish, Christian, and Muslim practitioners repeatedly reinscribed the notion that these three traditions shared the same (contested) prophecies, histories, and divinity. Ironically, these fictionalized tales of centrifugal origins are thus some of our best evidence of a centripetal model of the Abrahamic monotheisms. In this centripetal model, Judaism, Christianity, and Islam are not intrinsically bound together so much as they are persistently brought into relationship with one another by historical practitioners who insist that these three traditions share a divinity, revelation, and mythical-historical reality.

3.1 Pluralistic Centripetal Models

There has been a great deal of pushback in recent years against overly romantic visions of premodern ecumenism or *convivencia* (Stroumsa 2006, 3–6). When I say that local iterations of Judaism, Christianity, and Islam have often employed centripetal gestures, it certainly does not mean that historical practitioners embraced an egalitarian, ecumenical, or harmonious relationship. Yet we do occasionally encounter historical thinkers who sketched a shared history of the Abrahamic traditions in modes that were pluralistic or inclusive in very nearly a contemporary sense of those terms. That is, one does find historical practitioners who explicitly sought to imagine ways in which different Abrahamic communities could each authentically claim to represent the will of the same God by carefully coordinating the truth claims of multiple traditions in such a way that their diverse modes of religious life could plausibly be fit into a single account of sacred history.

Few progressive proponents of interfaith dialogue would take issue, for instance, with positions such as that expressed by the twelfth-century Yemenite Jewish thinker Natanel ibn al-Fayyumi[3] when he claimed that:

> Mohammed was a prophet to them [the Muslims] but not to those who preceded them in the knowledge of God [the Jews] . . . since [God] permitted to every people something which He forbade to others, and He forbade to them something which He permitted to others, for He knows what is best for his creatures and what is adapted to them even as a skilled physician understands his patients (Levine 1908, Judeo-Arabic 68, English 107)[4]

---

[3] I have tried to draw examples of these various patterns from as broad a historical and geographical area as possible because only a few specific periods and regions are generally known for these sorts of interactions – with the result that these well-known examples are frequently quarantined and dismissed as brief historical anomalies.

[4] In nearly every case, I direct the reader both to a copy of the source in the original language and an English language translation, so that students at every level of expertise can further explore each source if they wish. Wherever possible, I have taken English translations from full length translations of the primary source in question so that readers may read the quotation in its broader

As al-Fayyumi glosses in the words of the Quran: "'He sends a prophet to every people according to their language'" (Quran 14.4) (Levine 1908, Judeo-Arabic 69, English 109). In this rendering of Abrahamic history, both Muslims and Jews possess a true version of scripture from a single God. The obvious differences between these two prophetic testimonies reflect the particular needs of the recipients rather than any imperfection in their respective access to divine truth. By imagining the God of Abraham as a physician who sends individualized guidance to his patients according to their needs, this vision of sacred history allows for radical practical pluralism without undermining the notion that Jews and Muslims participate in a single spiritual reality governed by a single divine being. Instead, it combines Jewish and Muslim accounts of prophetic history into a single extended account that allows the basic truth claims of each to remain intact by limiting their scope of application.

One also encounters the claim that revelation refracted differently for different Abrahamic communities in the work of Muslim authors such as the thirteenth-century Andalusian mystic Abū 'Abd Allāh Muḥammad ibn al-'Arabī al-Ṭā'ī al-Ḥātimī (known as Ibn Arabi) who argued in his *Meccan Revelations* that each of the Abrahamic prophets and sages had been sent a version of revelation uniquely appropriate to his time and place:

> The article makes the word "religion" definite because all religion comes from God, even if some of the rulings are diverse. Everyone is commanded to perform the religion and to come together in it, that is, in the way upon which all agree. As for the rulings which are diverse, that is because of the Law which God assigned to each one of the messengers. He said, "To every one [of the prophets] We have appointed a Law and a way; and if God had willed, He would have made you one nation" (Qur'an 5:48). If He had done that, your revealed Laws would not be diverse (Arabic Yahia 1968, III.413; English Chittick 1989, 303)

Like al-Fayyumi, Ibn Arabi understood the diversity of revealed religion (both within Islam and among the other Abrahamic traditions) to reflect the needs of different communities at different moments. For Ibn Arabi, therefore, the revelations of Judaism and Christianity had neither been corrupted nor

---

context if they so choose. Where that was not practical because full translations were unavailable or difficult to access outside a specialized research university, I direct the reader to a translation from an accessible work of secondary literature that will serve as an introduction to the primary source. Where no translator is noted, I was forced to use my own translation. In the rare instance where no original source is cited, original language sources were in manuscript or preserved in limited run editions that are difficult to access outside the research university interlibrary loan system, and so not practical for classroom use. When these rare books are cited it is because they are freely available through Google books, archive.org, or Hathi Trust.

abrogated in the sense that they were subsequently abolished or repealed. Their own continuing but provincial manifestation of divine truth had simply been eclipsed by the brighter light of the Quran. As Ibn al-Arabi opined elsewhere in his *Meccan Revelations*:

> All the revealed religions [*shara'i'*] are lights. Among these religions, the revealed religion of Muhammad is like the light of the sun among the lights of the stars. When the sun appears, the lights of the stars are hidden, and their lights are included in the light of the sun. Their being hidden is like the abrogation of the other revealed religions that takes place through Muhammad's revealed religion. Nevertheless, they do in fact exist, just as the existence of the light of the stars is actualized. This explains why we have been required in our all-inclusive religion to have faith in the truth of all the messengers and all the revealed religions. They are not rendered null [*batil*] by abrogation – that is the opinion of the ignorant (Arabic Yahia 1968, III.53; English Chittick 1994, 125).

While Ibn Arabi certainly perceives a hierarchy of Abrahamic revelations – in which the Quran represents a brighter and more universal manifestation of God's truth than any of its predecessors – he simultaneously validates the truth value of diverse Abrahamic teachings and the unique ability of each to shed light on a particular facet of the divine.

Others were willing to acknowledge the truth value of other Abrahamic traditions without necessarily affirming their revelations. In his eighth-century Syriac work *Apology of Timothy the Patriarch Before the Caliph Mahdi,* for instance, the Nestorian Patriarch Timothy I offers the following account of the prophet Mohammad:

> Muhammad is worthy of all praise, by all reasonable people . . . He walked in the path of the prophets and trod in the track of the lovers of God. All the prophets taught the doctrine of one God, and since Muhammad taught the doctrine of the unity of God, he walked, therefore, in the path of the prophets. Further, all the prophets drove men away from bad works, and brought them nearer to good works, and since Muhammad drove his people away from bad works and brought them nearer to the good ones, he walked, therefore, in the path of the prophets. Again, all the prophets separated men from idolatry and polytheism, and attached them to God and to His cult, and since Muhammad separated his people from idolatry and polytheism and attached them to the cult and the knowledge of one God, beside whom there is no other God, it is obvious that he walked in the path of the prophets. Finally, Muhammad taught about God, His Word, and His Spirit, Muhammad walked, therefore, in the path of all the prophets.
>
> Who will not praise, honor, and exalt the one who not only fought for God in words, but showed also his zeal for Him in the sword? As Moses did with the Children of Israel when he saw that they had fashioned a golden calf

which they worshipped, and killed all of those who were worshipping it . . . And what Abraham, that friend and beloved of God, did in turning his face from idols and from his kinsmen, and looking only towards one God and becoming the preacher of one God to other peoples, this also Muhammad did (Syriac Van Roey 1946, 383; English Mingana 2009, 61–62).

While the Christian patriarch did not acknowledge the Quran as a new divine revelation, he was still willing to grant that Mohammad also founded a biblical religion of sorts. Timothy coded Mohammad as a second biblical Abraham, turning his people from idolatry to monotheism. In the early Islamic conquests, Timothy glimpsed the spirit of Moses as he ordered the idolatrous worshippers of the golden calf to death. Taken as a whole, Timothy argued that the precepts of Islam removed practitioners from bad deeds and brought them closer to correct conduct. Most importantly perhaps, the patriarch maintained that the teachings of Islam brought its adherents to knowledge of the One God (and even taught its adherents about Jesus and the Holy Spirit). In other words, Timothy maintained that Islam captured the spirit of biblical prophecy without a prophecy of its own because Mohammad "trod in the track of the lovers of God."

3.2 Critical Centripetal Models

While a minority of premodern Jewish, Christian, and Muslim authors embraced relatively pluralistic visions of a united Abrahamic prophetic history, many other religious thinkers sutured these communities together into a single historical imaginary in less ecumenical ways. As we see time and again, an author did not need to admire a fellow traveler in order to bind their two histories together into a single sacred story. In one common twist on the limited pluralism models analyzed above, for instance, many thinkers treated the prophetic traditions of rival Abrahamic movements as authentic but less than ideal prophecies issued by God to address less than ideal situations. It was not uncommon, for instance, for medieval Muslim scholars to portray the rigors of Hebrew Bible law as a particularistic divine punishment (or curative) for Jewish intractability. In his comment on Quran 16:124 in his *Commentary on the Mighty Quran*, for instance, the fourteenth-century Syrian exegete Abu al-Fidā 'Imād Ad-Din Ismā'īl ibn 'Umar ibn Kathīr (known as Ibn Kathir) portrayed the institution of the Jewish Saturday Sabbath as a concession to Jewish insistence:

There is no doubt that for every nation, God prescribed one day of the week for people to gather and worship Him. For this Ummah, he prescribed Friday, because it is the sixth day on which Allah completed and perfected His creation. On this day, He gathered and completed His blessings for his servants. It was said that Allah prescribed this day for the Children of Israel through his Prophet Moses, but they changed it and chose Saturday because it was the day on which the Creator did not create anything, as He had completed his creation by Friday. Allah made observance of the Sabbath obligatory for them in the laws of the Torah, telling them to keep the Sabbath ... Hence Allah says the Sabbath was only prescribed for those who differed concerning it (Quran 16:124) (Arabic Arafat 2005, 1031; English Abdul-Rahman 2009, 179).

In this twist on the notion that each nation received an individual prophetic prescription appropriate to itself, Ibn Kathir acknowledged that the Jewish people possess a legitimate divine prophecy that differs from the Quran, while denying that both prophecies possess equal claim to divine truth. Had the Israelites not stubbornly insisted on the seventh day as their holy day, God would never have commanded them to keep a seventh-day Sabbath with its requirements to rest. But since they insisted on celebrating the day on which God had already finished his work of creation, God produced an observance of ceasing and rest appropriate to that day. In this passage, the Hebrew Bible is treated as adhering to cosmological truth – rightly representing the unfolding history of creation and preserving rituals that echo that primordial history. But the Torah is also treated as a less than ideal blueprint for the moral life – a prophetic lifestyle that was adjusted to accommodate the contingencies of human characters and their limitations.

We also find a slightly less unflattering tale of divine accommodation in accounts such as the anonymous ninth-century Christian work, *Disputation of John and the Emir*, which suggests that the Hebrew patriarchs and prophets had to carefully tailor their revelations to avoid the pitfalls of an idolatrous age:

Abraham, Isaac, Jacob, Moses, Aaron, and the rest of the [Hebrew] prophets ... as [God's] intimates and confidants, they knew the truth. But there was the childish and uneducated state of the people of that time who were inclined and attracted towards a multitude of gods to the point of considering even pieces of wood, stone, and many other things to be gods, and erecting idols, worshipping, and even sacrificing to them. The holy ones did not want to give the errant an occasion to depart from the living god and to go after error. But cautiously they said that which is the truth: Hear, oh Israel, that the Lord your God, the Lord is one [Deut. 6:5]. For they truly knew that God is one and one divinity of the Father and the Son and the Holy Spirit ... But he is not, nor is he confessed [to be], three gods or three divinities, or by any means gods or divinities (Syriac Penn 2008, 83, English, 87)

In this case, the prophecies of the Hebrew Bible are explicitly recognized as "the truth." They are simply a "cautious" version of the truth tailored for an age in which humanity had a tendency toward polytheism and could not yet be told of a plural godhead without the risk of misunderstanding and error. According to this limited version of prophetic pluralism, the radical monotheism of the Hebrew Bible and the trinity of later Christian theology represent two different statements of the same truth – diverging in superficial presentation because each was shaped to account for the communal presuppositions of their own religious era.

While one might reasonably argue that Christian and Muslim scholars had a vested theological interest in carefully defining their relationship to the preexisting Hebrew Bible, we find this same type of centrifugal hierarchy in Jewish sources that represent the prophecies of Mohammed as a limited revelation sent by God for a sacred political-historical purposes. As the medieval apocalyptic midrash *Secrets of Rabbi Shimon bar Yochai*, for instance, characterizes the rise of Islam:

> When [the visionary] perceived that the kingdom of Ishmael would come (and exercise dominion over Israel), he exclaimed: "Is it not sufficient what the wicked kingdom of Edom [Christianity] has done to us that we should also (suffer the dominion of) the kingdom of Ishmael!? Immediately Metatron the [angelic] prince of the Presence answered him and said: "Do not be afraid, mortal, for the Holy One, blessed be He, is bringing about the kingdom of Ishmael only for the purpose of delivering you from that wicked one (i.e. Edom). He shall raise up over them a prophet in accordance with His will, and He will subdue the land for them; and they shall come and restore it with grandeur (Hebrew Jellinek 1967, III.78; English Reeves 2005, 78–80).

The prophecy of Mohammed is acknowledged here as a prophecy sent by the one God "in accordance with His will." The spread of Islam is also acknowledged as divinely ordained – as God himself "will subdue the land for them." Muslims are portrayed here as authentic followers of the Jewish God. Yet, the purpose of their prophetic movement has been severely circumscribed in this account. Rather than a universal prophecy intended to radically reorient human values, the Quran has been recast here as a politically expedient revelation composed to free the Jewish people from a difficult bondage under Christian rule. The God of Abraham is imagined here as having multiple subject communities and revelations – but they exist in a hierarchy of divine priorities with the Jewish recipients of the Hebrew Bible at the top.

3.3 Instrumentalist Centripetal Models

As we saw in the previous example, another common gesture was to treat other Abrahamic religions as an *instrumental* necessity for the unfolding of the divine plan. The most famous example of this dynamic is probably the fourth-century North African bishop Augustine of Hippo, who proposed that God maintained the Jewish people in their traditional observance through the Christian era so that Jews might act as a permanent witness to the nature of the Old Testament covenant:

> The Jews survive still, and for a special purpose: so that they may carry our books … A Jew carries the book which is the foundation of the faith for a Christian. Jews act as book-bearers for us, like the slaves who are accustomed to walk behind their masters carrying their books, so that while the slaves sink under the weight, the masters make great strides reading (Exposition of Psalm 56, Latin Migne 1864, 35.666, English, Boulding 2001, 110)

In a historical moment when the Jews as a people were increasingly being ascribed no role in Christian visions of ongoing sacred history, Augustine (re)inscribed both the Hebrew prophetic texts maintained by Jews and the traditional observance of Jewish practitioners as divinely ordained and necessary contributions to Christian salvation history (Fredriksen 2010). By denigrating Jewish authorities as enslaved scribes, Augustine ironically attests to the accuracy of their Hebrew texts – a claim that had come under attack by other thinkers who insisted that Jewish authorities had amended the Hebrew Bible to thwart Christian exegesis (Wollenberg 2019, 145–146). As Augustine puts it elsewhere, Jewish prophetic books are trustworthy because "what else is that people today but a certain library for Christians, which holds the law and the prophets as a witness" (Against Faustus 12:23, Latin Migne 1886, 42.266, English Teske 2007, 140). In reducing Jewish scholars to the neutral status of an inert object, Augustine could reimagine the Jewish people as "our" book bearers – claiming the Hebrew Bible as a Christian document and thereby establishing the Hebrew Bible as a point of overlap between these two Abrahamic traditions. Indeed, Augustine even inaugurated a disparaging form of revelatory pluralism when he argued that both Christian freedom from the law and continued Jewish observance of the old covenant were ordained by the same God, who had designated the Jews for the role of living books sinking under the weight of their exemplary Old Testament observances.

Though the best known, Augustine was far from the only thinker to propose an unflattering instrumentalist reading of another Abrahamic tradition. The twelfth-century Egyptian Jewish authority Moses Maimonides, for instance, argued that the teachings of Christianity and Islam had been ordained by God to prepare the world for the advent of the Jewish messiah by disseminating Hebrew prophecy and its basic truths:

> The intent of the Creator of the world is not within the power of man to comprehend, for His ways are not our ways, nor are His thoughts our thoughts. [Ultimately,] all the deeds of Jesus of Nazareth and the Ishmaelite [Mohammed] who arose after him will only serve to prepare the way for the

Messiah's coming and the correction of the entire world to serve God together as (Zephaniah 3:9) states: "I will transform the peoples to a purer language that they all will call upon the name of God and serve Him with one purpose." How will this come about? The entire world has already become filled with the mention of the Messiah, Torah, and *mitzvot*. These matters have been spread to the furthermost islands to many stubborn-hearted nations. They discuss these matters and the *mitzvot* of the Torah, saying: "These mitzvoth were true, but were already negated in the present age and are not applicable for all time." Others say: "Implied in the mitzvoth are hidden concepts that cannot be understood simply. The Messiah has already come and revealed those hidden [truths]." When the true Messianic king will arise and prove successful, his [position becoming] exalted and uplifted, they will all return and realize that their ancestors endowed them with a false heritage and their prophets and ancestors caused them to err (Mishneh Torah, Book of Judges 11:4, Hebrew and English Touger 1993, 613–616).

According Maimonides, neither Christians nor Muslims had received true prophecies. There is no revelatory pluralism in this account. And yet, Maimonides argues that these two religious movements were ordained by the one God for the education of humankind and were even foretold by the Hebrew prophets as part of sacred history. Like Augustine before him, Maimonides imagined his Abrahamic counterparts as carriers of the Hebrew Bible. He insisted that both Christians and Muslims knew the Hebrew Bible and its commandments. They simply misinterpret the status of the Hebrew Bible in the contemporary world – claiming that these commandments had been abrogated or were to be read allegorically. But even in their depreciation of the Hebrew prophets, Maimonides argues, Christians and Muslims nevertheless preserved and propagated the Hebrew prophetic ideals of God, revelation, commandments, and messianic redemption – bringing these ideals to stubborn and far-flung peoples who would not otherwise be reached by Hebrew prophetic truth. Through them, all the nations of the world were being improved in their morals, acclimated to the name of God, and prepared for a universal messianic age. In this vision of sacred history, the other Abrahamic communities do not possess prophetic traditions in their own right but they are nevertheless important servants of the God of Abraham – disseminating his true prophecies and ideals along with their own errors – and these messengers will ultimately "return" to God's fuller truth and be redeemed alongside the Jews.

Like the Christian and Jewish authors quoted above, Muslim authors likewise discussed the instrumental value of preserving biblical revelations and their interpretive traditions into the era of the Quran. The fifteenth-century Cairene scholars Ibrāhīm b. ʿUmar b. Ḥasan al-Biqāʿī (known as al-Biqaʾi), for instance, wrote a treatise gathering Islamic traditions concerning the continuing value of the Hebrew Bible (and the Gospels) as an ongoing source of sacred knowledge, entitled *Just Words on the Permissibility regarding Quotations from the Ancient Books*. In one section, for example, al-Biqa'i gathered a series of Muslim traditions in which Jews, Christians, and even a talking wolf, had confirmed the words of the Prophet or the authenticity of a religious tradition (Arabic in Saleh 2008a, 88–90) and demonstrated that Mohammed embraced teachings that dispelled doubt "from all the different kinds of human beings and creatures" (Arabic in Saleh 2008a, 90). The Hebrew Bible and New Testament in particular, al-Biqa'i argued, maintain continuing value for the purposes of moral "exhortation *(al-itti az* or *al-i tibar)*" (Saleh 2008b, 643). For as al-Baqa'i writes of the book of Jeremiah in his quranic commentary *Arrangement of the Pearls* it is "a style sublime in its rhetoric and exquisite in its tenderness; such is its beauty that it crumbles the livers, rends the hearts, makes eyes swell with tears" (English and Arabic Saleh 2008b, 636). While neither biblical texts nor their Jewish and Christian interpreters could be held up as an independent source of religious authority according to al-Biqa'i (Arabic Saleh 2008a, 91–92), their traditions could nevertheless be useful as an affirmation of God's will and a source of inspiration to true believers.

3.4 Models of Centripetal Triangulation

Although the forgoing examples mostly discussed relations between only two Abrahamic traditions, historical thinkers often triangulated between all three Abrahamic traditions in complex ways that implicitly affirmed different types of truth claims made by each tradition. An early medieval Christian source, The Armenian Chronicles of 661 attributed to Sebeos, for instance, imagines the rise of Islam as a spiritual reawakening of the children of Ishmael instigated by Jewish exiles who feared Christian oppression. According to this account, when the Byzantine emperor Heraclius exiled the Jews from Edessa, they traveled to the "sons of Ishmael" and "called on them to help them" (Armenian Abgaryan 1979, 135 English Shoemaker 2021, 63). To aid them in their cause:

> [The Jews] told [the Ishmaelites] of their hereditary kinship in the testament of the Scripture. Yet although they were able to persuade them of their close kinship, they could not achieve agreement within their multitude, because their religious practices divided them from each other. At that time a man appeared from among these same sons of Ishmael, whose name was Muhammad, a merchant, who appeared to them as if by God's command as a preacher, as the way of truth. He taught them to recognize the God of Abraham, because he was especially learned and well informed in the history of Moses. Now because the command was from on high, through a single command, they all came together in unity of religion and abandoning vain

cults, they returned to the living God who had appeared to their father Abraham. Then Muhammad established laws for them: not to eat carrion, and not to drink wine, and not to speak falsely, and not to engage in fornication. And he said, "With an oath God promised this land to Abraham and his descendants after him forever. And he brought it about as he said in the time when he loved Israel. Truly, you are now the sons of Abraham, and God is fulfilling the promise to Abraham and his descendants on your behalf. Now love the God of Abraham with a single mind, and go and seize your land, which God gave to your father Abraham, and no one will be able to stand against you in battle, because God is with you." (Armenian Abgaryan 1979, 135; English Shoemaker 2021, 64)

At which point, the new Muslim army arrayed itself in twelve camps according their lineages from the twelve sons of Ishmael (Genesis 25:13–16) and joined forces with the remnants of the twelve tribes of Israel to send a letter to the Byzantine emperor informing him: "God gave that land to our father Abraham and to his descendants after him as a hereditary possession. We are the sons of Abraham. You have occupied our land long enough" (Armenian Abgaryan 1979, 136; English Shoemaker 2021, 65). Although some later Christian sources would portray Jewish influence on Muhammad as nefarious and unwholesome, the Armenian Chronicle treated this development as both natural and divinely ordained.

According to this account, the sons of Ishmael had maintained their natural kinship associations with the biblical patriarchs but had lost the more important spiritual heritage that accompanied that legacy. When the sons of Isaac turned to their blood kin for aid in a time of loss and danger, they instigated a much-needed religious revival through which the sons of Ishmael "returned to the living God" who was their birthright since he had already "appeared to their father Abraham." While the chronicle does not acknowledge Muhammad as a prophet in his own right, it does recognize him as a preacher of inherited religious truth who was learned in biblical lore and who could teach others to "recognize the God of Abraham." Even Muslim military expansion is imagined here as a rightful claim on the Ishmaelites biblical patrimony instigated by Jewish exiles who naturally wished to return to the land of their forefathers. Indeed, this development is treated as divinely ordained, since we are told that through the conquest the biblical prophecy was fulfilled "[Ishmael's] hands against all, and the hands of all against him" (Genesis 16:22). While the author does not acknowledge Muslim prophetic claims, it does put Islam on equal footing with Judaism as a manifestation of the ancient biblical religion of Abraham. While in no way elevating Judaism and Islam to the level of Christianity, both the Jewish mission to the Arabs and the prophet Muhammad are treated as promoting forms of true piety capable of bringing their practitioners to knowledge of the living God. Pseudo-Sebeous thus elided the specificity of Jewish and Muslim religious claims in order to acknowledge these two traditions as a form of legitimate Abrahamic religion.

Other thinkers did the inverse – knowledgeably leveraging specific traditions from their Abrahamic rivals to triangulate a hierarchy of religious truth. The twelfth-century Jewish-heritage convert to Islam Samau'al al-Maghribi, for instance, utilized extra-biblical rabbinic traditions about the life of Jesus to demonstrate that Jesus was the Messiah who the Hebrew prophets had predicted would arrive and abrogate the law:

> We say to them: Is it not in the Torah that you have ... *Kingship shall not depart from the people of Judah nor the staff from amongst them until the Messiah has come* [Genesis 49:10] ... We then say to them: Do you not know that you once had a state and a kingdom up to the advent of Jesus, and that then your kingdom came to an end? If you do not have a kingdom today, it follows from the Torah that the Messiah has already been sent ... They cannot deny this without becoming absurd. So it follows from their own source, from the Torah, that Jesus the son of Mary is the Messiah they were expecting ... We say to them: What say you about Jesus the son of Mary? They will say: [Jesus is] the son of Joseph the carpenter by fornication; he learned God's great name and with its help used to impose his will upon many things. We say to them: Is it not true that, according to your best [midrashic] tradition, Moses was taught by God the divine name composed of forty-two letters with which Moses parted the sea and performed miracles? They cannot deny this. Then we say to them: If Moses also performed miracles by invoking the names of God, why do you believe in his prophethood and reject that of Jesus? (Arabic Perlmann 1964, 122–123, English 41–42)

While al-Maghribi's ultimate aim was to convince his former coreligionists that the Torah of Moses has been abrogated so that he might persuade them to accept Islam, he does so indirectly by advocating for Christian claims that Jesus was the Jewish Messiah heralded by the Hebrew Bible. Without embracing a redemptive Christology, al-Maghribi recognizes Jesus as more than simply a prophet. Jesus is acknowledged here specifically as the Jewish Messiah assigned by the one God to fulfill and abrogate the Law of Moses – thereby ushering in a radically new era in both Jewish and universal prophetic history. Moreover, the notion that the Christian era represented a new phase in prophetic history is demonstrated by embracing the post-biblical history of the Jewish people as a meaningful prophetic bellwether. The exile of the Jewish people from their land (in contradistinction to the promises of Genesis 49:10) demonstrated that the peoples of the world have entered a new era of history. The contemporary irrelevance of the Jewish mission is ironically established by treating the fate of the Jewish people as a sign for a universal prophetic history.

At the very moment that al-Maghribi denies the continuing relevance of the Torah of Moses, he affirms that the words of the Torah are true and cannot be gainsaid – only fulfilled. Yet al-Maghribi did not treat his Jewish contemporaries as mere remnants clinging to the Hebrew prophets but instead approaches later rabbinic tradition as another valid source of religious testimony. One can prove the prophethood of Jesus, for instance, by comparing rabbinic extrascriptural traditions about the lives of Jesus and Moses – in which both utilized the secret name of God to perform miracles. Even as al-Maghribi denied that Jews have understood their own stories about Jesus, he argued that these later rabbinic traditions can also be taken as reliable religious testimony.

Although many of these triangulations appear in (ostensibly) outward-facing polemic literature, other authors bore witness to the ways in which the claims of Abrahamic rivals also came to be woven into the imaginative cloth of internal thought and debate. In his *Book of Lighthouses and Watchtowers*, for instance, the tenth-century Karaite Jewish author Yaqub al-Qirqisani treated the rise of Christianity as just one Jewish heretical movement among many and his Muslim compatriots primarily as inconvenient witnesses to Jewish heresy. While internal polemic works often leverage the bogeyman of the outsider as a powerful rhetorical tool to shape internal orthodoxies, Qirqisani did not give Christianity and Islam even that privileged role. While the teachings of a minor Jewish thinker (with no living followers) who denied the validity of the scholarly Masoretic philological reading tradition were described dramatically as "evil doings," "harmful, shameful, and absurd to the utmost degree," (Arabic Nemoy 1939, 1.56; English Nemoy 1930, 388). Qirqisani reported mildly and ambivalently regarding Jesus:

> The Jews differ greatly in regard to Jesus. Some say that he claimed to be a prophet, and some deny it . . . . As for Benjamin (al-Nahawandi), I was told that he said that five Jewish men (fraudulently) claimed to be prophets, one of them being Jesus. He said: "To them refers the passage of the Scripture (Dan 11:14), 'Also the rebellious sons of thy people will lift themselves up to establish the vision, but they will stumble.'" As for some of the Karaites, they say that Jesus was a righteous man and that his way (of teaching) was the same as that of Zadok and Anan; but the Rabbanites went after him until they killed him, just as they sought also to kill Anan, although they could not do it. This is their way with everyone who attempts to oppose them (Arabic Nemoy 1939, 1.43; English Nemoy 1930, 365).

In Qirqisani's treatment, Jesus of Nazareth was characterized not as a religious rival but as an ambiguous Jewish type. Was Jesus among the "rebellious sons" of the Jewish people who became a prophetic pretender? Or was Jesus yet another righteous teacher seeking to return the Jewish people to biblical truth, persecuted by the rabbinic leadership because he denied their authority? Meanwhile, the later Christian religion instituted by "the Jew" Paul (Arabic Nemoy 1939, 1.44; English Nemoy 1930, 367) is indeed designated "utter heresy." Yet Qirqisani did not treat even the "heresy" of Paul as an alien religious tradition but instead described it as a recognizable amalgam of previous Jewish sects, "a combination of that of the Sadducees and that of the Qara'ians." (Arabic Nemoy 1939, 1.48; English Nemoy 1930, 377)

Meanwhile, Muslim theologians appeared throughout the essay primarily as gullible witnesses to Jewish heresy. Since Muhammad was a simple person not "accustomed to research and speculation, who would investigate the origins of Jesus's history, he acknowledged his miracles" just as his followers would continue to put a naive faith in implausible Christian evidence in their own times (Arabic Nemoy 1939, 1.45; English Nemoy 1930, 369–370). Muslims thus figured *Watchtowers* primarily as witnesses to different types of Jewish misbelief. As Qirqisani opines about a particular rabbinic tradition that he sees as particularly dangerous theologically: "If the Muslims only knew about this assertion of theirs, they would not need any other thing to reproach us with and use as an argument against us" (Arabic Nemoy 1939, 1.15; English Nemoy 1930, 331) In Qirqisani's account of the Abrahamic traditions, Christianity and Islam were melted into the history of the Jews' own confusion about the God of Abraham – becoming part of the history of "all the doctrines of the dissenters who appeared (among the Jews) down to the present time" (Arabic Nemoy 1939, 1.75; English Nemoy 1930, 391). Christianity and Islam were categorized as heresy and delusion, but they were in good company – part of a constantly reoccurring pattern of theological degeneration among the people of Israel themselves.

3.5 Centrifugal Relations and Collective Monotheism

A great deal of attention has been paid to the distinguishing, identity-defining function of polemic imagery like that described earlier. Certainly, Jews, Christians, and Muslims have found a great deal to criticize in each other – almost as much as they found to criticize among their own co-religionists. But I believe we have underestimated the *generative* force produced by these intercommunal debates about shared figures and concepts. Each new tussle over the Abrahamic legacy defined particular communal boundaries but it simultaneously contributed to a broader affirmation that the God of Abraham ruled over all communities – or at least all communities that mattered. When historical practitioners sutured the three Abrahamic traditions into these varied accounts of universal sacred history, they enchanted their world. Through a form of collective monotheism, such thinkers displaced the possibility of an existence beyond the boundaries of communal belief with a version of human history in which scriptural patterns had continued into quotidian time and the boundary between religious communities was not between believers and nay-sayers but instead marked different perceptions of the same irrefutable sacred phenomenon.

In this section, we will explore a single example of this phenomenon at length. When the fifteenth-century Portuguese-Italian Jewish thinker Isaac Abarbanel wrote Christian and Muslim histories and beliefs into his exegesis of the Hebrew Bible prophets, for instance, this collective account of the Abrahamic traditions allowed the author to depict the contemporary globe as overflowing with the story and faith of Abraham. In a historical moment defined by intense pressure and uncertainty for European Jewry, Abarbanel used the stories of Christianity and Islam to offer an account of sacred history in which Jews did not stand alone as the sole surviving torchbearers of Abraham. Instead, he claimed that both the Muslim descendants of Ishmael and the Christian descendants of Esau had been given continued access to sacred history because of their ancestral merit. Neither the genealogies of Ishmael nor Esau were taken out of the running for the greater Abrahamic blessing in Abarbanel's account. Long after the biological family of Abraham was split, God continued to recognize both peoples as descendants of Abraham and they were offered a share in the revelatory inheritance along with the descendants of their younger brother. As Abarbanel imagines the days before the Sinaitic revelation:

> The Holy One returned to the children of Esau and the children of Ishmael [before the giving of the Torah] but they did not accept the Torah and did not want it, while the children of Israel did accept it ... For there were those among the [the children of Esau and Ishmael] who were not prepared by nature to receive the Torah and the keeping of the commandments despite the fact that the children of Esau and Ishmael were from the seed of Abraham (Abarbanel on Deuteronomy 33:1, Hebrew Bar Ilan 2023,[5] English original)

Initially, the children of Esau and Ishmael would reject God's revelation as too onerous. But even that vital moment of rejection would not remove them from prophetic history. Both movements would continue to embrace the basic theological tenets of their Abrahamic lineage. As Abarbanel puts it regarding Christianity:

> Just as Esau and Jacob were joined in their father and faith, so the faiths of the Christians and the Israelites are joined since they have one father and all of them believe in the God of gods and all of them presume the reality of the

---

[5] Unless otherwise noted, Aramaic and Hebrew texts are cited according to the (mostly critical) editions in the Bar Ilan Responsa Project Database. All rabbinic texts cited are also available for free at sefaria.org.

First Cause and turn to it without worshipping the stars and higher powers and they have a single Torah between them since both upheld and accepted the true Torah of Moses (Abarbanel on Isaiah 35:10, Hebrew Bar Ilan 2023, English original).

By coding both Christianity and Islam as authentic Abrahamic movements that were prophesized about by the seers of Israel, Abarbanel was able to write a triumphant account of sacred history in which the lineage of Abraham and knowledge of the true God has already reached all corners of the globe. For as the author declared, "the prophet uses the term 'all nations' to refer to Edom and Ishmael because these are the two sects of faith of the nations and encompass all the inhabitants of the globe and dwellers of the earth in this day" (Joel 4:1, Hebrew Bar Ilan 2023, English original). Living in lachrymose times for the Jews, embracing Christianity and Islam as imagined sister movements allowed Abarbanel to write a more triumphant history in which the God of Israel was not merely the sponsor of a small and persecuted religious movement but had already been accepted as ruler of the world.

When Abarbanel wrote the three Abrahamic traditions into a single prophetic account of sacred history, it also served to telescope scriptural and historical time – scripturalizing all future events and giving prophetic meaning to the tides of contemporary life. In his complicated narrative, spread over multiple commentaries, Abarbanel told a story of sacred history in which the various offspring of Abraham made fateful choices that intertwined their destinies repeatedly at vital moments of history – so that they wove in and out of each other's communal lives in a tapestry of merit, corruption, and punishment. Some of these outcomes were inevitable, according to his account. The first parting of the ways between Judaism and Christianity, for instance, was ordained the moment Jacob and Esau received their respective blessings from their father Isaac. Since Jacob received the blessing of the first born, "the children of Israel merited divine intimacy and providence and the more elevated blessing." While Esau "merited the blessing of material benefits" so that "the Christians received material benefits" (Abarbanel on Isaiah 35:12, Hebrew Bar Ilan 2023, English original) and the mixed blessing of empire (Abarbanel on Isaiah 35:10).

But these early partings of the ways were not the end of the story, according to Abarbanel. From later biblical times through the Roman Empire to the medieval Mediterranean, a history of longing and rivalry would draw these Abrahamic inheritors together repeatedly in patterns of divinely ordained punishment and redemption. Thus, when the Israelites sinned in the days of the First Temple, it was the sons of Ishmael who were sent with their Ishmaelite leader Nebuchadnezzar to destroy Jerusalem and exile the people (Abarbanel on Joel 2:27). When the Jewish people once again fell into sin in the Second Temple period, the Roman descendants of Esau were assigned the task of exiling them (Abarbanel on Amos 1:3). But even as the children of Ishmael and Esau gained the upper hand, the seeds of their own undoing were being sown. God arranged for the soul of Esau to be reincarnated as a Jew in Roman Palestine called Jesus of Nazareth and the Roman children of Esau were quickly drawn to their reborn leader (Abarbanel on Isaiah 35:10) – tying the fates of Rome and Jerusalem together forever. Many centuries later, for instance, these ties would draw the Christians back to Jerusalem to conquer a place that contained "all the holiness of their religion" and the tomb of their Jewish founder (Abarbanel on Obadiah 1:1, Hebrew Bar Ilan 2023, English original). Doing so would enrage the Ishmaelites for whom Jerusalem was also "a holy city for God" (Abarbanel on Obadiah 1:1, Hebrew Bar Ilan 2023, English original) and Christians and Muslims would slaughter each other in great numbers – thereby simultaneously punishing both peoples for their roles in the previous destructions of the city (Abarbanel on Joel 4:1). Until the Ishmaelites would finally gather all the nations of the East to beat back a final Christian crusade (Abarbanel on Obadiah 1:1) and, in doing so, return the ten lost tribes of Israel to the holy land in the ranks of their global army (Abarbanel on Obadiah 1:18) – closing the circle of loss and exile that their own conquests had brought the Jewish people and ushering in the messianic age. By identifying Christians and Muslims as active and continuous participants in the Abrahamic story, Abarbanel was thus able to tell a global postbiblical history in which world events were ordained by the God of Israel to reward and punish his many followers from the seed of Abraham. In this version of global history, the Jewish people were not being blown about by random winds of happenstance but were instead a vital strand in a broader biblical tapestry in which the family of Abraham played out its fate through continents and centuries.

4 The Abrahamic Vernacular

4.1 What Is an Abrahamic Tradition?

Up to this point, we have been discussing Judaism, Christianity, and Islam as if they were discrete and cohesive entities that maintain a single unified identity over time. This metaphor certainly represents the most common way of thinking about these three traditions. But it is terribly not accurate. There is no single Jewish, Christian, or Muslim concept of revelation, prayer, or afterlife but always a plurality of perspectives within each tradition. Indeed, many contemporary scholars of religion would argue that there is no such thing as a singular Judaism, Christianity, or Islam (Satlow 2006; Anidjar 2009; el-Zein 1977).

Yet it is easy to fall prey to the diachronic illusion that religious traditions function like individuals. We reason by analogy that humans are born as discrete individuals who maintain a sense of continuous identity as they grow and change through interaction with the world. So all too often we approach modern religious movements as natural continuations of the ancient communities to which they lay claim. We imagine the emerging Hasidic movement of eighteenth-century Eastern Europe, for instance, as a direct outgrowth of the late antique Persian Jewish thinkers who produced the Babylonian Talmud. In doing so, we treat rabbinic Judaism as if it were literally born with the fall of the Second Temple and developed new character traits when it grew and migrated around the globe.

But the parallel is not exact. Traditions are not living entities. They have no existence beyond the constant regeneration provided by human maintenance. As any scholar of premodern history can attest, even the most vital and durable forms of human tradition degrade with unsettling speed if practitioners cease to continually reinscribe and preserve them. Whether a given historical community makes strong or weak appeals to a discursive tradition (Asad 1986; Baumgarten and Rustow 2011), the living practitioners themselves exist only in the context of their own moment and situation.

Far-flung communities within a given tradition are thus less like limbs on a biological body than heirs to a legacy. In many cases, these metaphorical beneficiaries are not even direct descendants. All too often, historical practitioners of a given tradition are more like distant cousins who have inherited an estate on the other side of the world. They are legitimate inheritors who seek to make use of a legacy that is nevertheless radically alien to their immediate conditions and circumstances. At any given moment, the Abrahamic traditions exist primarily (perhaps solely) in the lives of local practitioners who engage with a discursive legacy of religious language and motifs to navigate a particular time and place of their own.

This shift toward recognizing the lives and thoughts of human practitioners as the primary location of the Abrahamic traditions in any given historical moment is necessary but it is not sufficient. It is also important to rethink how we envision these historical practitioners navigated their lives in relation to the traditions of tropes and norms which we call Judaism, Christianity, and Islam. More often than not, historical actors are imagined drawing resources from within a single closed silo of tradition. Or perhaps they are depicted as torn between the discrete demands of two competing traditions – each tradition tugging the individual toward their side of the boundary line in an intellectual tug of war.

This is the point where scholars of religion fall into their own version of "the territorial trap" (Szpiech 2022). Experts in international relations have long warned against the intellectual dangers of uncritically accepting the nation state's fictive claims to effectively represent a homogenized social order within its territorial boundaries (Agnew 1994). This is true of geographic boundaries of religion but we also must be wary of accepting too literally the ideological territorial claims made by the Abrahamic monotheisms over the habits and thoughts of the practitioners who fall within their borders. Like other collective social formations, religious identity is simultaneously assigned to practitioners and performed by them. But these two schemas interact in ways that are often incongruent, messy, and even irreconcilable.

It is therefore vital that we look beyond this siloed model to attend to the subjectivity of the historical actors at play. That is, we must consider how individual practitioners "experience their place in the world, in contrast to how they are perceived by others, or how they are ordered within relatively rigid external systems" (Spector 2006, 358). While we cannot ever truly access the subjective experiences of individual historical practitioners, we can at least refocus our attention on reconstructing their locative perspectives. That is, we can refocus our study of historical Judaism, Christianity, and Islam to center the navigational strategies and intellectual bricolage of practitioners as they made their way in the world in dialogue with the legacy of a discursive tradition.

4.2 What Is Vernacular Religion?

Here we enter the realm of vernacular religion (Primiano 1995; Dash Moore 2022). For many decades, subject-centered reconstructions of religion were limited to studies of religion-from-below – investigations of folk religion or popular piety. In this model, lived religion was marginalized as a peripheral corruption of official religious norms. Mainstream or elite practitioners were assumed to participate in the "correct" beliefs and practices assigned to them by religious institutions. The concept of vernacular religion has invited us to explore how *all* practitioners variously encounter, interpret, and manifest religious traditions in daily life – both through and beyond institutional structures.

Vernacular religion thus most closely approximates the moment in which traditions live – as they are constantly (re)iterated and (re)inscribed by their practitioners. As a result, vernacular religion also represents the primary junction at which traditions grow and evolve. This is obviously true of the religious vernaculars adopted by communal authorities. But it is equally true of popular thought and practice. A great deal of what we now think of as normative Judaism, Christianity, and Islam emerged from the vernacular religion of lay practitioners.

This realization is important for our current purposes because the study of vernacular religion has demonstrated the extent to which lived religion is so often truly vernacular within local communities – crossing intra-communal boundaries in shared logics of religious common sense. The moment at which traditions are recreated is thus also often the moment when they are most closely entangled with the traditions of other communities. Through the subjectivity of historical practitioners, traditions merge and disentangle in a constantly changing pattern of configurations.

This Element argues that the Abrahamic monotheisms have been particularly prone to dynamics of vernacular entanglement. For when diverse practitioners participate in diachronic traditions that claim to describe the same God and historical figures, local logics of communal common sense generate an even stronger field of influence. That is, the very existence of shared motifs and referents between these three traditions has facilitated the co-construction of overlapping (if sometimes competing) religious imaginations. As these local conceptual landscapes are reabsorbed into their broader discursive traditions, this ever-changing kaleidoscope of historical entanglements has given birth to evolving forms of Judaism, Christianity, and Islam that are subtly but inextricably imbricated with one another by the lasting traces of different moments of vernacular religious common sense.

5 Models of Religious Common Sense

5.1 Unofficial Ritual Vernaculars

While communal overlaps in lived religious experience were certainly not limited to unofficial practices, vernacular religious cultures did often flourish just beyond the church, synagogue, or mosque door – in unauthorized communal practices of religious healing, rituals of supernatural protection, or pietistic practices. Late antique Jewish and Christian leaders, for instance, frequently felt compelled to protest against congregants who went to ritual experts from the other community for healing or supernatural aid.

The fourth-century archbishop John Chrysostom, for instance, famously exhorted the Christians of Antioch to stop frequenting Jewish healers. "When you get some slight illness," he complained, "will you reject [Christ] as your master and … desert over to the synagogues?" (Homilies against Judaizing Christians 8.6.10, Greek Migne 1891, 48.937, English Harkins 1979, 228). "When you accept their charms and incantations," he argued, "your actions show that you consider the Jews more worthy of your belief than God (Homilies against Judaizing Christians, 8.8.5; Greek Migne 1891, 48.940; English Harkins 1979, 236) … You profess you are a Christian, but you rush off to their synagogues and beg them to help you" (Homilies against Judaizing Christians, 8.8.9; Greek Migne 1891, 48.941; English Harkins 1979, 238). For Chrysostom, Christians who accepted Jewish healing were crossing a clear ideological boundary.

It is far from clear that the practitioners in question agreed. While scholars are sometimes wary of using Chrysostom's highly rhetorical sermonic discourses as a source of information about the realities of local social practices, his homily on intercommunal healing is particularly rich in practical details that suggest a particular social reality beyond the page. Chrysostom argued, for instance, that Christians seeking Jewish ritual healing must have felt as if they were violating communal standards because of the way they behaved when seeking intercommunal healing:

> The way you act when you get to the synagogue makes it clear that you consider it a very serious sin to go to that wicked place. You are anxious that no one notice your arrival there; you urge your household, friends, and neighbors not to report you to the priests (Homilies against Judaizing Christians, 8.8.8; Greek Migne 1891, 48.940; English Harkins 1979, 238).

While Chrysostom himself opposes intercommunal rituals of healing and imagines that his congregants feel guilty about the practice, he also describes in some detail a robust vernacular religious culture in which not only ill Christians but also their family, friends, and neighbors can be expected to support recourse to Jewish religious healers.

Contemporary Jewish sources depict a similar disconnect between the religious sensibilities of communal authorities and lay practitioners on the question of intercommunal healing. In one story widely repeated in late antique rabbinic literature (tHullin 2:24, Ecclesiastes Rabbah 1.8, yShabbat 14:4 (14d), yAvodah Zarah 2:2 (40d), bAvodah Zarah 27b), for instance, the nephew of the rabbinic authority Rabbi Ishmael sought to be healed in the name of Jesus:

> There was a case in which a snake bit Eleazar b. Dama. Jacob of Kefar Sama came forward to heal him in the name of Jesus Pantera (Jesus of Nazareth). But R. Ishmael would not allow him to do so. He said to him, "I shall bring proof that it is permitted for him to heal me." But he did not suffice to bring proof before Ben Dama dropped dead. Said to him R. Ishmael, "Happy are you, O Ben Dama, for you left this world in peace and did not break through the fence of the sages" (yShabbat 14:4 (14d); Hebrew Bar Ilan 2023; English Neusner 1991, 398)

Scholars often debate whether the earliest appearance of this story represents a historical trace of early Jesus followers with Jewish heritage – and what this account can tell us about the status of such individuals within the late antique

Jewish community (Schremer, 87–100). Yet, this narrative was frequently preserved and reproduced in rabbinic sources long after Jewish Jesus followers ceased to be an urgent social issue. In the later reception history of this tale, the story of Eleazar b. Dama thus circulated as a more generic story about the opposition of community authorities to the blurring of communal boundaries among lay practitioners of Judaism and Christianity. Like John Chrysostom, Rabbi Ishmael describes intercommunal rituals of healing as a violation of religious boundaries. Yet his nephew appears to be immersed in a vernacular religious culture in which such cross-cultural supernatural healing is not only practiced but is even religiously justified. When Eleazar b. Dama falls ill, there is a Christian healer close at hand willing offer his services – which suggests that community ties are already in place to facilitate such healings. More importantly, Eleazar b. Dama is neither surreptitious nor guilty about his recourse to a Christian healer. On the contrary, even in a moment of extreme stress, the dying man already has biblical prooftexts on the tip of his tongue to justify the practice of intercommunal healing. While the respective authorities in these accounts dismissed intercommunal healings as an obvious violation of their own religious standards, it is not at all clear that the rest of their communities agreed with that assessment. Instead, the practitioners they describe appear to understand these intercommunal healing practices as licit – even religiously justified – forms of supernatural aid.

Certainly, those who embraced intercommunal healing and supernatural protection did not treat these different streams of ritual knowledge as mutually exclusive or incompatible. Archeological remains from late antiquity suggest that both the users of supernatural protections and those who produced them often took an eclectic approach drawing on both Jewish and Christian traditions of ritual expertise (Nutzman 2022). One fifth-century couple from the Persian town of Nippur, for instance, went to multiple ritual experts to commission the four incantation bowls they would use to protect their new home and appear to have divided the work equally between the Jewish and Christian experts since two bowls are inscribed in (Jewish) Aramaic square script and two are written in (Christian) Syriac script (Ilan 2013). Indeed, the ritual idioms of late antiquity became so cosmopolitan that modern scholars often cannot definitively identify from which community the expert who produced a particular amulet or ritual formula hailed (Boustan and Sanzo 2017).

Nor was such eclectic use of supernatural aid limited to marginal or uncommitted practitioners. In one fifth-century narrative, for instance, the North African bishop Augustine tells the story of a pious woman from Carthage who sought healing from both a Jewish ritual expert and a Christian saint and received a miraculous cure:

When I was there recently, a woman of rank, Petronia, had been miraculously cured of a serious illness of long standing, in which all medical appliances had failed, and, with the consent of the above-named bishop of the place, I exhorted her to publish an account of it that might be read to the people. She most promptly obeyed, and inserted in her narrative a circumstance which I cannot omit to mention . . . She said that she had been persuaded by a Jew to wear next her skin, under all her clothes, a hair girdle, and on this girdle a ring, which, instead of a gem, had a stone which had been found in the kidneys of an ox. Girt with this charm, she was making her way to the threshold of the holy martyr. But, after leaving Carthage, and when she had been lodging in her own demesne on the river Bagrada, and was now rising to continue her journey, she saw her ring lying before her feet. In great surprise she examined the hair girdle, and when she found it bound, as it had been, quite firmly with knots, she conjectured that the ring had been worn through and dropped off; but when she found that the ring was itself also perfectly whole, she presumed that by this great miracle she had received somehow a pledge of her cure, whereupon she untied the girdle, and cast it into the river, and the ring along with it. (City of God 222; Latin Dombart and Kalb 2013, 578; English Dods 1881, 495–496)

Petronia is ultimately cured by the intervention of St. Stephen, who miraculously removes the Jewish curative from her body while the wearer is en route to his shrine. But for our purposes, it is interesting to note that Petronia had originally prepared a healing regimen that included both a Jewish ritual expert and a visit to a Christian shrine. Nor was she ashamed to bring the Jewish ritual cure on her pilgrimage to visit the saint. While St. Stephen would ultimately demonstrate his power over Jewish ritual expertise by removing the object from her body, Petronia apparently did not fear disapprobation or perceive the Jewish amulet as an illicit object that might interfere with a Christian pilgrimage – and, indeed, the pious practitioner in this story merited a miraculous cure despite her recourse to eclectic supernatural aid.

While the practitioners who embraced these unofficial intercommunal rituals did not leave clear evidence of their motives, religious authorities like those cited above described practitioners who adopted shared rituals because they had been drawn into a cross-cultural biblical imaginary. The aforementioned John Chrysostom, for instance, complained that his Christian congregants who "rush to their synagogues" (Homilies Against Judaizing Christians 6.6.6; Greek Migne 1891, 48.913; English Harkins 1979, 169) do so because "the Law and the books of the prophets are there (Homilies Against Judaizing Christians 6.6.8; Greek Migne 1891, 48.913; English Harkins 1979, 170) and "in the Law and the prophets [the Jews] have a great allurement and many a snare to attract the more simple-minded sort of men" (Homilies Against Judaizing Christians 6.6.9; Greek Mignes 1891, 48.913; English Harkins 1979, 171).

Being able to offer direct access to the ancient language of the Hebrew prophecies bestowed a certain mystique on Jewish practitioners in the eyes of Chrysostom's congregants, according to the bishop. As did their practice of rituals which Chrysostom's congregants imagined to be identical with those of biblical times – a presumption that Chrysostom himself vehemently denied. "What is it that you are rushing to see in the synagogue of the Jews?" he complains "Tell me is it to hear the trumpeters [play the ram's horn shofar]?" (Homilies Against Judaizing Christians 4.7.4; Greek Mignes 1891, 48.881; English Harkins 1979, 92). "God explained how the trumpets were to be used for he went on to say 'You will sound them over the ... the sacrifices," Chrysostom argues. "But where is the altar? Where is the ark? Where is the tabernacle and the holy of holies ... Did you lose all those and keep only the trumpets? ... Do you Christians not see that what the Jews are doing is mockery rather than worship?" (Homilies Against Judaizing Christians 4.7.6; Greek Mignes 1891, 48.881; English Harkins 1979, 93). If Chrysostom's analysis of the situation is correct, local Christians who turned to Jewish experts for healing were drawn to their Jewish compatriot's facility with Hebrew biblical prophecies and their knowledge of ancient biblical rites that had been lost to Christian communities. While Chrysostom denied that late antique Jews were living an authentic biblical lifestyle, those who sought supernatural aid were apparently drawn into these intercommunal encounters by what they perceived as the Jews' special access to ancient biblical knowledge and rites.

One might imagine that this biblical mystique would only work in one direction – as the Jewish community accrued the prestige of lost biblical knowledge. But in the story of Elazar ben Dama who wishes to be healed in the name of Jesus above, we also encounter inverse rabbinic claims that Christian biblical interpretation constituted a dangerous allurement to the Jewish community. In the version of this story that appears in the late antique midrash Ecclesiastes Rabbah 1:8, for instance, the passage reports that Christian biblical teachings are like the beautiful harlot of Proverbs and a good rabbinic Jew must obey the injunction to "distance your way from her and do not approach the door of her house" (Proverbs 5:8). The passage then prefaces the story of Elazar ben Dama seeking to be healed in the name of Jesus with the pronouncement "because of this ["allurement"] Elazar ben Dama the nephew of Rabbi Ishmael died" (Ecclesiastes Rabbah 1:8). To illustrate the ways in which biblical discussions between Jews and Christians can become a source of intercommunal enticement, Ecclesiastes Rabbah details an exchange between a certain Rabbi Eliezer and a Christian in the marketplace of Sepphoris. The story begins as Rabbi Eliezer retrospectively wracks his brains to discover what he has done wrong to deserve a particular misfortune (in this case, being arrested by the Romans). To help him discover what hidden sin the pious rabbis might have committed to deserve these troubles, one of his students suggests "Perhaps one of the heretics [Christians] said a word [of Torah] before you and it was alluring to you?" To which Rabbi Eliezer responds with the following story:

> Heavens! You have reminded me. One time I was walking up the boulevard in Sepphoris. And a certain man came up to me, Jacob of Sikhnaya was his name, and he said a word [of Torah] in the name of a certain man [Jesus] and I enjoyed the teaching. The teaching was:
> "It is written in your Torah 'do not bring the wages of a sex worker or the price of a dog [into the house of the Lord]' (Deut 23:18). What is the ruling regarding them?"
> I said to him, "They are forbidden."
> He said to me, "They are forbidden for an offering, but for destruction they are permitted."
> I said to him, "If so, what should one do with them?"
> He said to me, "One should make bathhouses and latrines from them."
> I replied, "You have spoken well!" And for a moment I forgot the ruling [to distance oneself from their biblical interpretations].
> When he saw that I appreciated his words, he said to me, "So a certain man [Jesus] taught me: 'They came from filth and to filth they will go.' As it says in scripture, 'From the wages of a sex worker they were gathered and to the wages of a sex worker they will return' (Micah 1:7). Let it be a latrine seat for the public."
> I took pleasure [from the teaching], and for this reason I was arrested (Hebrew Bar Ilan 2023, English original).

According to this passage, Jews like Elazar ben Dama were being drawn into intercommunal healing by the enticements of Christian biblical interpretation. The passage then goes on to illustrate the allure of Christian biblical interpretation by recounting an exegetical discussion between a local Christian and a famous rabbi. In this discussion, the Christian interlocutor quotes only from the Hebrew Bible sources (citing Deuteronomy and Micah) and restricts his discussion to topics of shared interest. The Christian simply offers the rabbi a novel interpretation of the Hebrew Bible verses in question. Only once he has captured the admiration of his Jewish listener does Jacob share that his inspiring teaching came from none other than Jesus of Nazareth. In this passage, the enticement of Christian biblical interpretation lies in the fact that it is indistinguishable from Jewish interpretation. Even a rabbi might happily take away new insights about shared texts without any sense of discomfort to mark the event in his memory. Indeed, even after Rabbi Eliezer recalls the discussion and realizes retrospectively that he has transgressed the rabbinic ruling forbidding engagement with Christian biblical interpretation, the rabbi apparently remembers the encounter with pleasure (using words of pleasure and allurement throughout his recounting). Jewish practitioners are drawn toward the ritual world of Jesus and his followers, the passage implies, by a shared appreciation of biblical interpretation drawn from the Hebrew prophets. In other words, both of the late antique religious authorities cited here maintained that Jewish and Christian practitioners were being drawn into intercommunal vernaculars of healing and supernatural aid through shared scriptural vernaculars of biblical interpretation and ritual.

5.2 Ritual Vernaculars at the Margins

To say that such practitioners shared a scriptural vernacular did not mean, of course, that all participants believed identically about the scriptural traditions in question. In accounts of shrines and other semi-official religious spaces shared by Jews, Christians, and Muslims, for instance, one witnesses a variety of ways in which practitioners from multiple communities could construct disparate but interlocking scriptural accounts of a single powerful site. In some cases, visitors from different Abrahamic communities did appear to agree on the history and purpose of a site. In one fourteenth-century travelogue from Jewish Cairo, for instance, Yitgaddal the Scribe describes Muslims and Jews praying to the same God in roughly the same manner at the tomb of Aaron (Exodus 7:1; Quran 20:29–32) in Petra:

> Many come to bow down and prostrate themselves. The gentiles [*goyim*, i.e. the Muslims] maintain the place in great purity and for the honor of the prophet [Aaron], peace upon him. They pay respect to the Jews and honor them and allow them to enter to prostrate themselves and to pray there. May the Lord answer their and our prayers and the prayers of his nation Israel. Amen. (Hebrew Ilan 1997, 135; English Bousek 2018, 27).

According to Yitgaddal, both the Muslims who maintain the tomb and the Jews who visit it honored the same scriptural figure of Aaron and prostrated themselves to the one God at his tomb. While practitioners must have come to the shrine inspired by slightly different accounts of Aaron, each drawn from their own traditions, Yitgaddal appears to harbor no doubt that both communities honor a single scriptural figure and pray to the same God. On the contrary, Yitgaddal expects God to answer equally "both their and our prayers."

In other cases, multiple communities might come together to worship at a single site for the same reason – but offer slightly different accounts of the scriptural narrative in question. As the fifth-century church historian Salamanes Hermias Sozomenus (known as Sozomen), for instance, described interdenominational gatherings held at Mamre where Abraham was said to have been visited by three angels after his circumcision (Genesis 18):

> Here the inhabitants of the country and of the regions round Palestine assemble annually during the summer season to keep a feast … Indeed, this feast is diligently frequented by all nations: by the Jews, because they boast of their descent from the patriarch Abraham; by the Greeks (hellēsi), because angels there appeared to men; and by Christians, because he who for the salvation of mankind was born of a virgin, manifested himself there to a godly man. This place was moreover honored fittingly with religious exercises. Here some prayed to the God of all; some called upon the angels, poured out wine, burnt incense, or offered an ox (Ecclesiastical History, 2.4, Greek Hussey 1860, 117, English Nutzman 2022, 71–72).

In late antique Mamre, Sozomen reports, many nations worshipped in parallel to honor the appearance of angels to the patriarch Abraham. Yet each community emphasized a different aspect of the biblical tale. Jews called upon the ancestral merit of their patriarch Abraham. Christians emphasized an early Christian tradition that Christ appeared to Abraham at Mamre along with two angels. (As Sozomen put it, Christians celebrated the fact that "here the Son of God appeared to Abraham with two angels who had been sent against Sodom and foretold the birth of his son.") While local Greeks simply came to honor the appearance of angels to a human being. Jewish and Christian versions of the Mamre story remained subtly incompatible in this account – as Jews were unlikely to concede that Christ had ever appeared among the angels that visited Abraham. Yet Sozomen also claims that all visitors honor the site "fittingly with their religious exercises." As in Yitgaddal's account of the tomb of Aaron in Petra, moreover, both Jews and Christians at Mamre are acknowledged here to worship a single shared deity, "the God of all."

In a third set of cases, practitioners from different communities could not possibly have held congruent perceptions of the powerful site in question. Christian pilgrims to medieval Palestine, for instance, mentioned various ways in which local Jewish women (along with their Muslim counterparts) participated in rituals that these Christian authors understood to be devoted to the Virgin Mary. Thus, one fifteenth-century pilgrimage from Cologne, Arnold Von Harff, reported:

> From Bethlehem we travelled eastwards to seek the Holy City [Jerusalem]. Close behind this monastery is a cave in which our blessed Lady hid with Christ, her son, when Herod caused all the innocent children to be massacred [Matthew 2:16]. If pregnant women, who wish for quick delivery, take a spoonful of this earth mixed with wine or water they are said forthwith to be delivered. If women at childbirth, find their milk run dry and partake of it,

then forthwith the milk is said to return. This earth is fetched by the heathen [Muslim] and Jewish women, who put great trust in it (German von Groote 1860, 162, English Letts 2017, 189).

It is likely that Muslim visitors to the milk grotto did indeed attribute its powers to the shared scriptural figure of Mary, as they did at other Marian shrines throughout the region (Albera 2019; Cuffel 2003). It is less clear how Jewish women would have imagined the site. While it is certainly possible that the participation of Jewish women at the grotto was a figment of Von Harff's imagination, there is a long history of Jewish women unofficially entering Christian and Muslim spaces where Jewish men could not or would not do so. A contemporaneous fifteenth-century travel account by Rabbi Meshullam of Volterra, for instance, attests that Jewish women in nearby Hebron knew all sorts of decorative and financial details about the mosque built at the grave of the patriarchs because "many of them go into the mosque" when their male relatives do not (Hebrew Yaari 1948, 69; English Adler 2004, 186). The question is what might have drawn Jewish women to the grotto. It is possible that foreign visitors to the area were right to claim that some local Jewish women honored Mary not as the mother of the messiah but simply as a pious "kinswoman" (Limor 2007, 222). Certainly, local Jews venerated many other later historical figures who did not appear in the Hebrew Bible, including Joshua ben Perachia who was often imagined as a teacher of Jesus in premodern Jewish traditions (Reiner 1998). While Jewish Arabic biographies of Mary from the region portray a pious Jewish mother trapped by the machinations of evil men and the technicalities of the rabbinic legal system[6] – an image that may well have touched Jewish women. Alternately, the milk grotto may have been a multifaceted women's site similar to a nearby tomb shrine on the Mount of Olives in Jerusalem that Jewish sources claimed held the remains of Huldah the prophetess, Christian visitors attributed to the woman saint Pelagia, and Muslim materials insisted preserved the remains of the female Sufi mystic Rābiʿa al-ʿAdawiyya al-Qaysiyya (Limor 2007). Whatever the case, such sites drew together practitioners from different Abrahamic communities around the healing powers even of religious figures who did not appear in shared scripture – further intertwining the scriptural vernaculars of these communities beyond the ancient horizons of shared scriptural writings.

Shared sites and practices also entangled the post-scriptural religious lives of Abrahamic practitioners in another way. It was not uncommon for

---

[6] See, for instance, the stories of Mary's youth in the thirteenth-century manuscripts JTS ENA NS 32.5 and T-S NS 298.57 (Judeo-Arabic and English Goldstein 2023, 76–77 and 81–82, respectively).

observers from Abrahamic communities to interpret the ritual activities of other Abrahamic communities in scriptural terms. This was true even when the practices in question were undoubtedly new innovations. In the eleventh century, for instance, the Persian traveler Nasir-i Khusrau reported regarding the Dome of the Rock in Jerusalem:

> Now, the men of Syria, and of the neighboring parts, call the Holy City (the Bait al Mukaddas) by the name of Kuds (the Holy); and the people of these provinces, if they are unable to make the pilgrimage (to Mecca), will go up at the appointed season to [the Dome of the Rock complex in] Jerusalem, and there perform their rites [such as processing in a circle] ... as is customary to do (at Mecca on the same day). (Le Strange 1975, 88)

According to Khusrau, local Muslims had adapted the rituals of the Meccan hajj to the Dome of the Rock in Jerusalem – approaching the ancient stone at the center of the site with rituals developed for the Ka'aba in Mecca. Yet when this same ritual is described by a thirteenth-century Jewish observer, Rabbi Jacob, he imagines that local Muslims are honoring the site of the lost Jewish Temple with the rites of the ancient Israelites:

> Round the *even shetiah* [the foundation stone], the Ishmaelite Kings have built a very beautiful building for a house of prayer and erected on the top a very fine cupola. The building is on the site of the Holy of Holies and the Sanctuary ... The Moslems gather there on their holy days in crowds and dance around it in procession as the Israelites used to do on the seventh day of the festivals (Hebrew Eisenstein 1926, 67, English Adler 2004, 118–119).

When he witnessed the medieval pilgrimage rites developed by his Muslim contemporaries, Rabbi Jacob saw an echo of the ancient practice of circling the Temple altar in *hakkafot* on the seventh day of the Sukkot harvest festival – a ritual that late antique rabbinic literature attributes to biblical times. In the report of Rabbi Jacob, rabbinic tales of biblical times have become entangled with medieval Muslim practices to create a novel sort of biblical tableau in which one can witness the historical descendants of the biblical Ishmael honor the lost Temple of Solomon with ancient Israelite rites.

While communal practice at shrines or other sites of supplementary piety were not prescribed in the same way that other kinds of liturgy might be, the influence of the cross-cultural religious vernaculars developed in these shared spaces could nevertheless be both multifaceted and far reaching – ultimately encompassing not only communal practice but the thought of the religious authorities themselves. One of the best documented examples of this phenomenon was the spread of Sufi pietism among the Jews of Egypt from the thirteenth through fourteenth centuries under the auspices of the Maimonides family. From the late twelfth through

fourteenth centuries, Sufi mysticism spread rapidly among Egyptian Muslims and
many Jews were drawn to the pietistic movement. Some Jews attended Sufi
institutions regularly. Thus, the fourteenth-century wife of a certain Bashir the
Bellmaker could complain that "her husband was completely infatuated with life
on the mountain with [the Sufi master Yusuf al-'Ajami] al-Kurani" and "goes up
the mountain and mingles with the mendicants" regularly. Indeed, she reports that
he has begun pressuring her "to sell their house and leave the Jewish community
to stay on the mountain" with the families of the master's other disciples (Goitein
1953; Judeo-Arabic, 47–48; English, 48–49). Others adopted a variety of pietist
practices from ritual ablutions to various forms of ritual abstinence (Russ-
Fishbane 2015). While educated Egyptian Jews read Sufi literature both in
Arabic (Zsom 2015) and in Arabic transcribed into Hebrew characters (Miller
2023), as well as writing their own Sufi treatises in a Jewish idiom (Fenton 1995).
Thus far, the Jews of Egypt did not necessarily differ from their coreligionists in
other places. Jews throughout the Mediterranean and Middle East became
involved with Sufi teachers and circles (Kraemer 1992) and one of the best
known works in the rabbinic canon has been identified a Jewish-Sufi work
(Lobel 2013).

What sets the Egyptian example apart is the extent to which the Jewish
community left an explicit record of the scriptural vernacular at work in this
movement. The thirteenth-century leader of the Egyptian Jewish community
Abraham Maimonides, for instance, insisted that local Jews were only
(re)adopting the biblical "customs that have been transferred to the Sufis of
Islam" (Rosenblatt 1938 Judeo-Arabic 222 and English 223). As the author
elaborates elsewhere:

> The purpose of [the law] is that the nations imitate us and follow our law, as
> a single nation follows its leader, [according to the verse] "And you shall be
> unto Me a kingdom of priests [and a holy nation]" (Ex. 19:6) . . . Such that our
> wisdom and beloved customs have been hidden from us and reappeared in
> other peoples on account of our sins (Judeo-Arabic Dana 1989 152 and
> English Russ-Fishbane 81).

As in the pilgrimage accounts above, Abraham Maimonides saw his Muslim
compatriots as preserving lost biblical rites that had been lost among the Jews
through laxity and sin. The mystical and ascetic innovations of the Sufi movement were thus recoded by their Jewish viewer as a window onto the world of
the ancient Hebrew prophets. As Maimonides elaborates:

> [The Hebrew prophets adopted] the costume of "the true prophets" by attiring
> themselves in the garment of rag and suchlike garment(s) of the poor resem-
> bling the dress of the Sufis in our days, and (also to their assumption of)

restriction in food to the point of being content with crumbs and the like, as he said: "And with crumbs of bread" (Ezek. 13:19) … And do not regard as unseemly our comparison of that to the behavior of the Sufis, because the Sufis imitate the prophets and walk in their footsteps, not the prophets in theirs. (Rosenblat 1938, Judeo-Arabic 321 and English 322).

Like many lay practitioners involved in practices of supplementary piety, this rabbinic leader read the behavior of an adjacent Abrahamic community as a form of living text – an embodied commentary on the lost world of the Hebrew scriptures.

This perception of Sufi biblicism was not limited to questions of practice, however. In the theological work of Abraham's fourteenth- to fifteenth-century descendant David ben Joshua Maimonides, for instance, one can discover a nearly seamless integration of Sufi teachings and biblical evidence. In a treatise outlining Sufi teachings about the spiritual power of music, for instance, Maimonides draws his proofs and examples from Hebrew Bible accounts of king David and the prophets (Fenton 1982). Elsewhere, the scholar quotes heavily from Sufi texts but substitutes Hebrew Bible prooftexts for the original Quranic verses in his rendering of these texts (Hofer 2014, 373).[7] In such passages, contemporary Sufi thought is treated as identical with biblical teachings – to the extent that one can be prooftexted by the other. In the Sufi-Jewish movement in medieval Egypt, we thus encounter evidence of a long-standing and multifaceted scriptural vernacular that encompassed both lay practitioners and community leaders and became embedded in both communal practice and elite biblical interpretation.

5.3 Scholars Reading Together

The members of the Maimonides family were far from the only scholars to participate in intercommunal scriptural vernaculars. Quite the contrary. If the stories preserved in elite sources are any guide, Jewish, Christian, and Muslim authorities often read sacred literature together – seeking out religious knowledge from one another both in person and from the page.[8] At their most basic, such encounters were limited to a joint exploration of the philological facets of scripture – as scholars worked together to determine what a particular scriptural text meant on the most literal level. In one medieval Jewish narrative, for instance, we are told that the head of the rabbinic academy in Baghdad sent a student to the Christian patriarch to inquire about the Christian community's reading of a phrase in the biblical book of Psalms:

---

[7] For accounts of Jewish authors using and translating Quranic prooftexts intact, see Decter 2006.

[8] The historical record suggests that Abrahamic scholarly elites also read other kinds of learned literature together across religious boundaries in ecumenical "philosophical friendships" (Stroumsa 2019, 96–101) and study circles (Brann, 7).

> The Nagid (R. Samuel ibn Nagrilah) may his soul rest in Paradise, recounted
> this in his work *The Book of Contentment*, after having cited at length Christian
> commentaries, how R. Matzliah ben al-Basaq *Dayan* (rabbinic judge) of Sicily,
> wrote him upon his return from Baghdad, an epistle in which he . . . recounted
> among other things how one day in the gathering, the verse שמן ראש אל יני ראשי
> was mentioned and the attendees disagreed over its interpretation. R. Hayya
> bade R. Matzliah to go to the Christian Catholicos to ask him what commen-
> tarial traditions he has for this verse. This was odious to him (R. Matzliah). He
> (R. Hayya Ga'on) of blessed memory, upon seeing how distressing the behest
> was for R. Matzliah, the Gaon of blessed memory reproached him saying "our
> pious forefathers and ancestors who are our paragons would inquire regarding
> languages and their explanations from members of different religions, even
> from shepherds and cow-hands, as is well known and passed down." He
> (R. Matzliah) arose and went to him (the Patriarch) and asked him. He
> (the Patriarch) told him (R. Matzliah) that their [tradition] in Syriac was
> משחא דרשיעא לא עדי רישיה. (Dubovik English 99–100, Judeo-Arabic 100).

This passage cannot be read as a historical account as we would understand that
term, although the basic facts about Hai Gaon's attitude toward non-Jewish
knowledge do appear to be accurate. (We know, e.g., that this historical leader
of the Babylonian academy did in fact incorporate Muslim sources into his
writings on Jewish religious law (Stampfer 2020).) Nevertheless, this anecdote
about early eleventh-century Baghdad comes to us not from an eyewitness but
from the end of a thirteenth-century North African commentary on *Song of Songs*
by Rabbi Yosef ibn 'Aqnin. Indeed, the author himself emphasizes the geographical and chronological distance between his own writings and this incident when
he reports that he himself found the story in an eleventh-century book by the
Andalusian scholar and communal authority Samuel ibn Nagrilah (known as
Shmuel ha-Nagid). At the same time, the very length and geographical scope of
this story's reception history serves to normalize the practice of consulting other
Abrahamic communities about shared scripture in its own way. The story appears
in an epilogue in which Ibn 'Aqnin seeks to explain his own practice of citing
non-Jewish sources in his biblical commentaries. He then relates that the great
sage and community leader Samuel ibn Nagrilah was wont to cite Christian
commentaries in his own writings. Defending his own practices of intercommunal citation then led that leader of Andalusian Jewry to record a story he heard
about the illustrious Babylonian leader Hai Gaon in which that head of the
rabbinic academy also consulted Christian sources on biblical issues. Finally,
the illustrious Hai Gaon is said to have cited the long-standing precedent from
previous Jewish sages on this issue. If Ibn 'Aqnin is to be believed, it was thus an
age-old global practice for Jewish scholars to consult with their Abrahamic
compatriots on questions of biblical philology. At the very least, one North

African Jewish scholar saw it as plausible that many famous rabbis would consult their Abrahamic counterparts to help resolve interpretive disputes within the Jewish community.

Whether or not we accept the tale of Hai Gaon and the Catholicos as historically accurate, it is far from the only story in which leaders from one Abrahamic community consult members of another Abrahamic community to resolve an internal interpretative dispute about the language of scripture. One dramatic narrative in this pattern can be found, for instance, in an exchange of letters between the renown fourth-century scholars and church leaders Jerome of Stridon and Augustine of Hippo – a discussion that Jerome would come to refer to as "the ridiculous 'gourd' debate" since the debate concerned the correct Latin word to describe the vine mentioned in the Hebrew text of Jonah 4:6 (Jerome to Augustine Epistle 81, Latin Hammon 1865, 33.275, English Dods 1872 316).

It is well-known that Jerome went to some lengths to seek out Jewish teachers and sources as he prepared his famous Latin translation directly from the Hebrew Bible (Williams 2008a and 2008b). This would not be the end of Jewish involvement with Jerome's Vulgate translation project, however. For when this new translation was introduced into the lectionary, Augustine complains that it generated a translational free-for-all in which Christian readers began to consult their own Jewish neighbors and amend Jerome's rendering of the Hebrew text accordingly. As Augustine reports, for instance:

> A certain bishop, one of our brethren, having introduced in the church over which he presides the reading of your version, came upon a word in the book of the prophet Jonah, from which you have given a very different rendering from that which had been of old familiar . . . to all the worshippers . . . for so many generations in the church. Thereupon arose such a tumult in the congregation . . . denouncing the translation as false, that the bishop was compelled to ask the testimony of the Jewish residents (it was in the town of Oea). These, whether from ignorance or from spite, answered that the words in the Hebrew were correctly rendered in the Greek version, and in the Latin one taken from it . . . The man was compelled to correct your version in that passage as if it had been false translated as he desired not to be left without a congregation – a calamity which he narrowly escaped (Epistle 71, Latin Hammon 1865, 33.242, English Dods 262–263)

In reply to this letter from Augustine, Jerome answers with some disgust that Augustine and his flock should consult with *more* Jews if they doubt his translation abilities:

> For I have not followed my own imagination, but have rendered the divine words as I found them understood by those who speak the Hebrew language. If you have any doubt of this in any passage, ask the Jews what is the meaning

of the original. Perhaps you will say, "What if the Jews decline to answer, or choose to impose upon us?" Is it conceivable that the whole multitude of Jews will agree together to be silent if asked about my translation, and that none shall be found that has any knowledge of the Hebrew language? Or will they all imitate those Jews whom you mentioned as having, in some little town, conspired to injure my reputation? . . . But if your Jews said, either through malice or ignorance . . . that the word is in the Hebrew text which is found in the Greek and Latin versions, it is evident that they were either unacquainted with Hebrew or have been pleased to say what was not true, in order to make sport of the gourd-planters (Epistle 75, Latin Hammon 1865, 33.253, English Dods 298–299).

In this exchange, two prominent Christian scholars debate which of "their" Jews (as Jerome puts it) knows the Hebrew Bible best. If we accept Augustine's account of the church in Oea, moreover, lay readers also consulted with local Jews and even used Jewish linguistic authority to overrule their own bishop concerning the correct reading of the Hebrew Bible. Whether this particular linguistic rebellion ever took place in the North Africa town of Oea, the exchange between Jerome and Augustine describes multiple examples of such linguistic consultations taking place across numerous geographical locations – thereby normalizing the presence of Jews as linguistic participants in Christian biblical interpretation.

To say that scholars from different communities sometimes acted as philological partners in the interpretation of scripture does not mean that such interactions were always cooperative. On the contrary, many of these philological entanglements were highly ambiguous in their tenor. Writing toward the end of the Reconquista, for instance, the fifteenth-century retired Spanish cardinal Juan de Segovia argued with deep ambivalence that European Christians should stop making war with Muslims but instead conquer this misguided heresy through peaceful dialogue with its adherents.[9] To further this project, de Segovia sought to learn Arabic and produce a more accurate translation of the Quran that could be used to inform such exchanges. To this end, de Segovia writes with delight that he had succeeded in persuading a local Muslim leader to join him in his remote mountain retreat to produce a new vernacular translation of the Quran:

> This man answered that he could not come, because he was not competent, and because it would not yet be possible [for him to collaborate]. Then it pleased God to fulfil my wish, a wish which complied with the glory of His

---

[9] For a detailed exposition of Juan de Segovia's position on interfaith dialogue and its role in the spread of global Christianity, see the Latin and English editions of his 1454 letter to Nicolas Cusa in Wolf 2014, 252–261.

name. My family and friends guaranteed the inviolability of his [Yca's] person and the salary that he had asked for his efforts. Then, on the 4th of December 1455, he arrived at the place where I live, in the priory of Aiton, in the diocese of St. Jean de Maurienne, a man who was of great renown among the Saracens of Castile Yca Gidelli *faqih* of Segovia, accompanied by someone belonging to his sect (Wolf 2014, Latin 328 and English 188–189).

Gidelli and his companion appear to have taken the translation work seriously – reportedly spending twelve hours a day for the next three months pouring over scholarly books to produce a correct translation of the Quran into Castillian Spanish. As their host reports, "I saw that [the Muslim scholars] had many books without vocals, especially books by their doctors, which he called expounders of the Qur'an, and which he consulted when uncertain" (Wieger, Latin and English 106). In the final fourth month, Gidelli and de Segovia read sat together and read over the Arabic and vernacular translation side by side to ensure that the final work was accurate and de Segovia understood it. The resulting translation must have been satisfactory to its Muslim authors, as well, because they requested that a second copy to be made for their own use. In this example, a fraught and ideologically complicated philological project gave birth to a new vernacular rendering of scripture that was literally shared between two communities.

Other accounts suggest that such linguistic intimacy could develop even between scholars who entered these relationships with openly polemic intent. The eleventh-century leader of the Andalusian Zahiri (literalist) school Abū Muḥammad ʿAlī ibn Aḥmad ibn Saʿīd Ibn Ḥazm, for instance, was known as a sharp polemicist against the accuracy of extant Jewish and Christian scriptures – as evidenced by the lengthy title of his famous *Treatise on the Obvious Contradictions and Evident Lies in the Books Which the Jews Call the Torah and in the Rest of Their Books, and in the Four Gospels, All of Which Establish That These Have Been Distorted and Are Different from What God, Mighty and Exalted, Revealed.* Yet Ibn Hazm did not keep his distance from his Jewish and Christian interlocutors. Within the pages of the treatise itself, Ibn Hazm records linguistic discussions with scholars from other Abrahamic communities in which he felt he achieved the upper hand, such as a debate with the famous Shmuel ha-Nagid about whether the Hebrew term *ahoti* (my sister) used by Abraham to describe his wife Sarah in Genesis 20:12 always meant "sister" or could also be interpretative expansively to mean "female relative" (Pulcini 1998, 60). Nor do these anecdotes appear to be fabricated for rhetorical purposes. The eleventh-century Andalusian biographer Abī 'al-Ḥasan ʿAlī ibn Bassām claimed that Ibn Hazm was devoting so much time to Hebrew scriptures and Jewish interlocutors that his cousin wrote the scholar a rebuking letter after

Ibn Hazm was installed as head of the Zehirite movement to complain that the scholar was spending so much time in the house of the *hazzan* (Jewish cantorial reader) that he was neglecting his duties (Adang 1996, 95). As we have seen throughout this Element, Abrahamic interlocutors did not need to agree about the issues at hand in order to share a scriptural vernacular.

The exegetes who engaged in these linguistic entanglements did not always spell out their motives. However, the accounts we do possess often express concern that the scholar's own knowledge of scriptural tradition might be inaccurate or incomplete in some way and evince hope that scholars from other Abrahamic communities might have textual witnesses or philological information that will complete or refine their own knowledge. One ninth-century letter written by the Catholicos Timothy I of Baghdad to the bishop Mar Sergius of Elam, for instance, attests to the frustration both scholars experienced with the biblical manuscripts available to them and captures Timothy's rather romantic hopes that better editions will be found in other Abrahamic communities. Timothy begins his letter by detailing a textual correction project he has undertaken to produce a more authentic versions of the Syro-Hexapla (a Syriac Bible translation that drew on the Septuagint column in Origen's ancient critical edition of the Hebrew Bible) – and promises Mar Sergius his own long-awaited copy of the new edition. Throughout his account, Timothy complains of the textual errors that riddle the biblical texts available to him. The new copy has "endless differences from what [we already] possess," he reports, and "even the exemplar from which we copied had problems [in the Greek]" (Letter 47, Syriac Heimgartner 2012 79, English Butts 2021, 126). In the second half of the letter, Timothy relays a report that the Jews of Jerusalem have laid their hands on Hebrew manuscripts of the biblical text preserved from the times of the biblical prophets themselves:

> We have learned from some Jews, worthy to be believed, who now recently became disciples of Christianity, that ten years ago some books were found near Jericho in a dwelling in a mountain. They said the dog of an Arab man who was hunting went into a cleft after some game and did not come out. Its owner went after it and found a chamber in the mountain, in which there were many books. That hunter went to Jerusalem and relayed this to the Jews. Many of them came, and they found books of the Old Testament as well as others in Hebrew script. Since the one who told me about this knows the script and is literate, I asked him about certain verses that are adduced in our New Testament as coming from the Old, but there is no mention at all of them in the Old Testament, neither among us Christians nor among those Jews. He told me that there is, and they are found in those books that had been discovered there . . . That Hebrew man told me: "We found a psalter among those books that has more than two hundred psalms." I have written concerning these matters to

them. I think that these books were perhaps placed by the prophet Jeremiah, Baruch, or someone else ... when the prophets learned through divine revelation of the captivity, plunder, and burning that would come upon the people because of their sin ... they hid these books in the mountains and caves, and they buried them so that they would not burn in fire and not be plundered by captors. (Letter 47, Syriac Heimgartner 2012 80, English Butts 127).

While he himself is immersed in the quotidian scholarly frustrations of trying to reconstruct an accurate copy of scripture from the existing manuscripts, Timothy imagines that the Jewish community has access to more perfect manuscripts than his own. Thanks to their linguistic prowess in Hebrew and geographical proximity to ancient biblical sites, Timothy believes that the Jewish community of Jerusalem has come into possession of uncorrupted biblical manuscripts from the times of the prophets. To Timothy, it is obvious that these newly discovered biblical books "are more trustworthy than those [current] among the Hebrew and those among us" and the patriarch longs to read them with "a burning fire in my heart" (Letter 47, Syriac Heimgartner 2012, 81 English Butts 128). In the hopes of gaining access to this esoteric source of biblical truth, Timothy has been badgering local Jewish converts and writing to the Jewish community in Jerusalem though he has "not received any answer from them about this" (Syriac Heimgartner 2012, 81 English Butts 128). For Timothy, the Hebrew speakers of the Jewish community are the answer to his philological prayers – an imagined source of lost biblical knowledge to which only they have access.

Several centuries later, we find a slightly ironic inverse echo of the patriarch's tale in the work of the thirteenth-century Catalonian rabbi Moses Nachmanides. In various places, Nachmanides explains why he quoted from a Christian Syriac edition of the apocryphal biblical book *The Wisdom of Solomon* in his sermons and biblical commentary. As Nachmanides understood the provenance of this text it had been preserved and translated by Christians but actually recorded an ancient Jewish tradition of what the biblical "King Solomon of blessed memory said in his book called The Great Wisdom of Solomon" (Hebrew Marx 1921, 59, English original). As Nachmanides explained:

We find another book called The Great Wisdom of Solomon which is written in difficult Aramaic and the Christians have translated it from that language. I believe that this book was not arranged by the Men of Hezekiah, the king of Judah, but that it went with the Jews to Babylon orally and there they fixed it in their language [of Aramaic] (Sermon on Ecclesiastes of 1266–1267, Hebrew and English Marx 1921, 60)

According to Nachmanides, the fact that this Christian witness to biblical wisdom was written in a form of Aramaic (Syriac) demonstrates that the Christians had preserved a lost Jewish interpretative tradition from the time of the Bible. For as Nachmanides explains in the introduction to his commentary on Genesis: "Everything that was transmitted to Moses our teacher through the forty-nine gates of understanding was written in the Torah explicitly or by implication in words, in the numerical value of the letters or in the forms of the letters" (Hebrew Bar Ilan 2023; English Chavel 1999, 10). But "these hints cannot be understood except from mouth to mouth [through the oral tradition which can be traced] to Moses, who received it on Sinai" (Hebrew Bar Ilan 2023; English Chavel 1999, 11).Therefore, much of the Bible's wisdom remained locked until the biblical "King Solomon, peace be upon him, derived it all from the Torah, and from it he studied until he knew the secrets of all things created" (Hebrew Bar Ilan 2023, English Chavel 1999, 12). This esoteric biblical wisdom was then preserved in sources such as "the Aramaic translation of the book called *The Great Wisdom of Solomon*" for in it "is written ... 'I have prayed, and the spirit of wisdom was given to me and I have called out and the spirit of knowledge came to me'" (Hebrew Bar Ilan 2023; English Chavel 1999, 12). According to Nachmanides, therefore, "all of this [hidden wisdom] Solomon knew from the Torah and he found everything in it – in its simple meanings, in the subtleties of its expressions and its letters and its strokes" (Hebrew Bar Ilan 2023; English Chavel 1999, 13). In other words, Nachmanides was willing to embrace this extra-biblical work transmitted by Christians because he believed that it recorded an esoteric biblical tradition that had been lost to the Jewish community. In this case, Christians were imagined as the bearers of Jewish books – so that a Jewish scholar could turn to the Christian library to reclaim lost Jewish exegetical knowledge.

Yet scholars did not only turn to other Abrahamic communities to recover ancient knowledge or lost scriptural traditions. Sometimes interpreters claimed that they worked together with experts from other Abrahamic communities simply to refine their understanding of the philological meaning of vital texts written in ancient languages that were no longer perfectly understood. In the preface to one translation of the Pentateuch produced for Coptic Christians in 1242 CE, for instance, the author details how (and why) he created a base text by sitting together with a Jewish colleague to produce a correct edition and interpretation of the tenth-century rabbi Sa'adiah Gaon's annotated (Judeo-) Arabic translation of the Hebrew Bible:

> While studying the holy Torah, I found its Arabic versions that I had become acquainted with differing from one another in some of the expressions. As a consequence, they deviated in their meaning. I scrutinized this matter with care and found it to be due to the translators from one language into another during the ages ... However, as I perused the translation of the learned Rabbanite Sa'id al-Fayyumi [hereafter Saadiah], I satisfied myself owning

to his style that he is the most preferred of all translators and the most eloquent interpreter among the people of his confession … Thus I copied his version in what follows this preface and with the intention of editing it most accurately. For this purpose, I summoned to my aid one of the most notable Israelites, whose name is stated at the end of this copy. He had memorized the text and recalled its words skillfully. Further, he was well versed in the study of its expression, its recitation, and everything related to the interpretation of its meaning, and also grasped its underlying intention. In his hand he held a copy in Hebrew letters, from which he read aloud in Arabic. In my hand I held the present copy in Arabic letters, which is Saadiah's translation that I intend to transcribe … What is more, I had at my disposal a number of commentaries of Christian, Jewish, and Samaritan provenance. (Vollandt 2018 Arabic 4 5 and English 9)

In this passage, we encounter an example of scholarly collaboration that approaches religious pluralism as we understand the term. In Muslim Egypt, two Arabic-speaking Abrahamic minorities work together without any apparent power dynamics between them to produce the best possible translation of a shared book, drawing on their own scholarly expertise and commentaries produced by a variety of Abrahamic communities – Christian, Jewish, and Samaritan. There is no romanticism in this account and no search for lost knowledge. The author of this preface was simply dissatisfied with the linguistic renderings of the Bible available to him and sought out the best possible translation tradition – even though that translation was produced by an expert from a different Abrahamic community. The author is willing to turn to a Jewish expert to help him with this work because he believes that he and his compatriot are fundamentally in agreement on some level concerning the nature and meaning of "the Holy Torah." Here the notion of a shared scriptural vernacular is literalized. Two scholars from different communities sit together to read a biblical translation aloud in a shared oral vernacular but using texts written in different scripts – so that they are reading the same book but in two distinct communally inflected editions.

5.4 Scholars Learning Together

Although linguistic entanglements were common, scholars also learned from one another in more substantive ways. Sometimes interreligious discussion was formalized. The medieval institution of the *majlis* (an intermural theological or philosophical salon that took place in Islamicate societies), for instance, represented a forum in which wider communal dialogues or debates took place regularly. In some cases, a community *majlis* (pl. *majalis*) might be quite pluralistic. As one traveler to tenth-century Baghdad supposedly complained:

> At the first session I attended, I saw a *majlis* which included every kind of group: Sunni Muslims and heretics, and all kinds of infidels: Majus, materialists, atheists, Jews and Christians. Each group had a leader who would speak on its doctrine and debate it. Whenever a leader arrived, from whichever of the groups he was, the assembly rose up for him, standing on their feet until he sat down . . . When the *majlis* was jammed with its participants, and they saw that no one else was expected, one of the infidels said, "You have all agreed to the debate, so the Muslims should not argue against us on the basis of the sayings of their prophet, since we put no credence in it, and do not acknowledge him. Let us dispute with one another only on the basis of arguments from reason, and what observation and deduction will support." Then they would say, "Agreed." Abu Umar said, "When I heard that, I did not return to that *majlis*. Later someone told me there was to be another *majlis* for discussion, so I went to it and found them involved in the same practice as their colleagues. So I stopped going to the *majalis* of the theologians and never went back" (English Griffith 1999, 62).

According to Abu Umar Ahmad ibn Muhammad ibn Sa'di, tenth-century Baghdad hosted multiple theological *majalis* in which Jews, Christians, and Muslims were relatively equal participants. The leaders of each community were honored with the practice of rising before a scholar. A non-Muslim could open the debate. Most importantly in a society with an official dominant religion, all participants had agreed to argue from the grounds of reason rather than religious authority. In the relatively humanistic and pluralistic scholarly culture of medieval Baghdad, such ecumenical *majalis* may well have taken place regularly (Kraemer 1992).

In its idealized form, a *majlis* could be conceived as a form of genuine religious learning, elevating its participants and their understanding through sincere dialogue. Thus, the ninth-to tenth-century Muslim theologian Abu Hassan al-Ash'ari in reported to have declared:

> In dialectical debates and disputations one should seek to get closer to God, the exalted. They should serve as a way to worship Him and to fulfil His commands . . . When these are lacking, disputations have no reason except greed, obstinancy, or glee in defeating the opponent and overcoming him. Other animals, such as the stallions of camels, rams and roosters, share this drive to conquer" (English Stroumsa 1999, 70–71).

While their animal instincts might urge participants in a *majlis* to argue for the sake of winning, al-Ash'ari presses those who engage in such dialectic debates to treat the discussions as an opportunity to get closer to God.

Although one might imagine that only those with the political upper hand would feel free to adopt such a serene approach to interreligious dialectic, similar sentiments are attributed to a certain Father George in a Christian account of a twelfth-century disputation in Aleppo:

Come now, let us take into consideration these religions and laws. The Sabian has a book and a law, and in like manner the Jew, the Christian, and the Muslim. Let us then draw a short sketch of each of these books and laws separately and examine them according to the rules of reason; and whichso-ever book shall indicate the nearest affinity to the divine and creating nature, let that be considered the true religion which was necessarily established by God. (Arabic Bodleian Library MS. Marsh 581 and Marsh 512, English Alexander Nicoll 1816, 431)

It may be taken as a given that Father George approached this ecumenical search for truth with a firm conviction that his own tradition would emerge as the true religion. Yet the monk also presumes that all of the Abrahamic participants in this dialogue serve a single God. More importantly perhaps, he posits that they each share at least an overlapping vision of that one God's "divine and creating nature" that they can collectively use to assess the precepts and scriptures of each tradition. In their most idealized form, the *majalis* are thus described as an opportunity to debate issues of shared concern amongst groups who embraced analogous or overlapping worldviews.

In other cases, these debates became acrimonious – particularly when they were shaped by local power dynamics. One manuscript fragment from Egypt, for instance, describes a tenth-century session in the vizier's weekly *majlis* in which Jews from various sects were invited to defend an Arabic translation of the Jewish prayer book but came away feeling humiliated and ridiculed:

When the most illustrious vizier Ya'qub ibn Yusuf, may God sustain his high station, showed me a translation made by a certain Jewish translator of the "Book of Prayers and Blessings" following the prescribed laws, which he translated from the language of Hebrew into Arabic language and script, neither he nor the company of thinkers – consisting of litterateurs who deal with Kalam [theo-logical dialectics] and philosophy as well as physicians present at the session in which religions are discussed, [all of whom] meet regularly at his court – ought to have vilified, ridiculed, and scorned the entire [Jewish] nation [as they did] (Cohen and Somekh 1990, Judeo-Arabic 290 and English 292).

This decidedly disgruntled account captures the ambiguous nature of such *majlis* encounters. This particular *majlis* session subjected a religious minority to an uncomplimentary disputation infused with the power of a political leader and the religious majority – although it should be noted that it appears everyone left the session with nothing hurt beyond their pride. At the same time, the author describes a prolonged encounter in which a wide variety of local intellectuals were introduced to a vernacular translation of the Jewish liturgy – and thus became familiar with the prayers and blessings of that religious minority. In this case, a certain level of religious intimacy was achieved between two

Abrahamic communities through a less than irenic exchange of views. As we have seen time and again in this Element, entanglements of religious learning and practice can develop in a wide variety of environments and affective relationships.

Some of the most robust Abrahamic scholarly networks were even built by researchers working at cross purposes – inspired by ultimately incompatible goals and commitments. Early modern European Christian Hebraists, for instance, worked together with their Jewish compatriots to produce a significant library of new editions and translations of traditional Jewish religious literature that ultimately offered more accessible versions of these texts to both Christians and Jews. As the German Jewish scholar Shabbetai Bass described the utility of these works for Jewish readers in his 1680 bibliography of Hebrew literature:

> [This work] includes a list of many books that were translated from the Holy Tongue into the Latin language . . . Some books were written in both the Holy Tongue and Latin – they are the work of non-Jews. This demonstrates the potency of the Holy Tongue – for all nations make every effort to learn and to write books in the Holy Tongue and to translate works from the Holy Tongue into other languages. The wise person will appreciate the considerable utility of this section. I would have you know that I have listed the dates in which they were published according to their [i.e. Christian] era. (Hebrew Bass 1806, 107a; English Boxel et al. 2022, 3)

At a time when Jewish scholars themselves were increasingly producing vernacular translations and annotated editions of rabbinic literature for more novice Jewish readers, this influx of Christian sponsorship and printing fell in with the Jewish spirit of the times.

At the same time, early modernity saw a growing conviction among Christian scholars that knowledge of Hebrew and Aramaic rabbinic traditions was necessary both to understand the New Testament and to convey its truth successfully to a Jewish audience. As the Scottish Calvinist minister John Dury put it in a 1649 pamphlet on the issue:

> Concerning the Oriental Languages, and the writings of Jewish Mysteries, which are found therein; this is their prerogative before all other Tongues and Writings of the World. That the first Oracles of God were uttered therein; that the fundamental Principles of all true Worship and Religion towards God, were first made known, by them to the world . . . for it is unquestionably true, that at first all these things have been peculiar to the Jews, and from them by degrees were propagated the rest of the Nations. Therefore, no doubt much respect is justly due unto those Languages; and if their hidden treasures were opened, it is most certain, that a great addition of Wisdom would thereby redound unto the rest of the world. (spelling modernized from Dury 1649, 14–15).

> This usefulness of the Oriental languages, and of the Jewish Rabbinical
> writings, hath moved many in the reformed Churches abroad, to apply
> themselves of late unto the study thereof, with much diligence and industry
> (spelling modernized from Dury 1649, 16).

Through annotated study editions and translations of rabbinic texts, Dury
argues, the "Jewish Mysteries" were likewise made available to Christian
scholars and "their hidden treasures were opened" to the many who sought to
"apply themselves . . . unto the study thereof."

In one joint Jewish-Christian production of a vocalized study edition of the
Mishnah in 1646, we encounter an interesting of example of the ways in which
different communal visions came to intersect in the production and consump-
tion of these texts. While the edition was printed by a Jewish press in
Amsterdam and extant copies of the work have been found marked up by
Jewish readers, copies of the work were also purchased by Christian readers
ranging from a New England minister to Prince Augustus Fredrick, Duke of
Sussex (Sclar 2022, 293). The project began as a joint endeavor of Rabbi Jacob
Judah Leon Templo, a local Jew of Portuguese descent, and the Dutch minister
Adam Boreel. According to his friends, Boreel supported the two scholars for
seven or eight years – going into considerable debt in the process – while they
shared a house and worked together to produce a vocalized edition of the
Mishnah. As Jacob Judah Leon Templo would describe these years in his
preface to the printed Mishnah:

> During my time in Middelburg . . . in my home in the company of a respectable
> youth, I greatly desired to devote myself to . . . understanding the words of the
> sages of the Mishnah . . . Sitting then peacefully together as brother in deep
> communion, busy with understanding their words with all of our strength, to
> know how Israel should follow all the commandments and precepts, innumer-
> able times we came upon difficult and obscure passages which we could not
> understand because of the lack of vocalization, and only with great difficulty
> could we follow and grasp their meaning. But then the noble lord said to me,
> "Why do you slacken, it is the time for divine labor, go forth Leon, following
> the footsteps of the holy men and the judges as our holy rabbis whose names are
> signposts for the sake of the oral law. Do not abandon their legacy . . . this is
> a timely task . . . this glorious work is upon you, to make lighter or even to
> eliminate the burden of those who study the Talmud. Gird up your loins as
> a man and make signs with your fingers, [vowel] points of silver on every word
> so at to situate it in its precise place" (Hebrew MSS Bibliotheca Rosenthaliana
> Ros.1899 G28, Popkin and Katz 1988 English 152–153).

In this public account of their studies, Templo obscures the fact that his study
partner was Christian. Yet the interfaith nature of the venture comes through in
his account in other ways. The rabbi emphasizes that (any expectations to the

contrary) the two scholars lived "peacefully together" and worked "in deep communion" – while not bound by ethnic or religious kinship, they were "*as* brothers." If Templo's account is accurate, this sense of shared purpose was actively cultivated by Boreel who agreed that they were working to "know how Israel should follow all the commandments and precepts" and called it a "divine labor" to "make lighter or even to eliminate the burden of those who study the Talmud" so that the modern reader should not "abandon their legacy."

Boreel's protestations may have been sincere – certainly, they moved Templo to considerable scholarly efforts. Yet the desire to preserve and clarify the rabbinic legacy was not Adam Boreel's only purpose in pursuing this joint project. As Boreel described his broader goals to Samuel Hartlib in a 1646 letter that coincided with the publication of the vocalized Mishnah, it would "help the Jewish people" to produce:

> Latin versions of the Talmud and the traditions in the Midrashim so that we may discourse with them, since we are ignorant of the beliefs of the Jews; and publish in Hebrew and vernacular languages used by Jews refutations of all the foundations the Jews have relied on from time immemorial until today (Latin Van der Wall 1989, 254, English original)

By his own admission, Boreel was sincerely interested in understanding and disseminating the languages and the traditions of the Jewish people. But he dedicated himself to this task because he believed that fostering Christian understanding of Jewish thought would facilitate the conversion of European Jewry. According to the reporting of his friends, Boreel did not see these two goals as incompatible. As John Durie reported the double purpose of the Mishnah project in his own 1646 letter to the aforementioned Samuel Hartlib, the new study edition was produced:

> To the end that both the Common sort of Jews might know what the Constitution of their Religion is, and also that the Learned sort of Christians upon the same discovery might be able to know how to deal with them for their Conviction (spelling modernized from van der Wall 1988, 147).

Whether Boreel also revealed his dual purpose to his rabbinic partner remains unclear. Yet the intercommunal nature of the project was certainly not an accident. When it came time to publish the new study edition, more Jewish and Christian scholars were drawn into the undertaking. The two Dutch Christians who financed the printing did not leave a detailed record of their motivations. Yet we do have a detailed account of the thought process from the Jewish editor and printer, who was chosen according to John Durie because the best way to reach both audiences would "be to publish the Mishnaioth . . . first under the name of some Jew; because if it should be put forth under the name, or by the industry of any Christian, it would not be of credit among [the Jews]" (spelling modernized from van der Wall 1988, 147). For this reason, the famous rabbi Menasseh ben Israel was brought on board to further annotate the text and supervise the printing. According to his preface to the edition, Menasseh ben Israel undertook the publication because he saw a great need for such a study text in contemporary Jewish circles:

> I saw many of the most wise and learned of my people stuttering over the pronunciation of many words instead of being precise. Few comprehend the conjugation of the verbs and laws of accentuation, nor the pronouns, and so do not know their right from their left. I said to myself in my heart, the time has come to serve God and to open an entry to students who have been reading for days and years, to make it easier for them with pointing and signs to lighten the burdens, for the meanings are hidden and sealed. (Hebrew MSS Bibliotheca Rosenthaliana Ros.1899 G28, English Popkin and Katz 151).

As Hebrew became an increasingly arcane language and many converted Jews returned to Judaism after the inquisition, the Jewish community was in need of such study editions of rabbinic literature that offered additional linguistic cues and annotation to assist the study of this ancient text. While Menasseh ben Israel did not publicly announce the mixed background of the project, that does not mean that he was not privy to the details. The rabbi himself was a correspondent and study partner of many Christian Hebraists connected to Boreel. It may therefore be telling that his preface echoes the language adopted by his silent Christian partners as he writes of lightening the burdens of the student to uncover the hidden mysteries of the rabbinic tradition. It is impossible to prove to what extent the participants in this project worked in true harmony of purpose and to what extent they saw their working partners as deluded. Whatever their individuals motives, these Jewish and Christian scholars produced a shared religious text of considerable depth and spent years of scholarly intimacy in the endeavor.

5.5 (Extra)-Scriptural Vernaculars

It is hardly surprising that centuries of such entangled encounters between both lay practitioners and scholars left their marks on Jewish, Christian, and Muslim traditions. Researchers have already documented in depth the ways in which the exegetical traditions of these three traditions often became intertwined in relation to shared scriptural figures such as Cain and Abel, the family of Abraham, Joseph, or Mary (Kugel 1999; Gregg 2015; Baumgarten 2022). But these shared scriptural vernaculars also took on life of their own – generating common mythologies that ventured far beyond the scriptural texts that inspired them.

In this section, we will explore this phenomenon in relation to a single lesser-known example.

Many Jews, Christians, and Muslims across a wide geographic and chronological range were convinced that the scriptural Noah had possessed at least one book of secret supernatural knowledge that he subsequently passed down through the generations. This notion could be said to have a direct scriptural basis in only the most tangential sense. The Second Temple *Book of Jubilees* (canonized only by the Ethiopian Orthodox Church and the Beta Israel) records that Noah wrote down everything that he knew about medicine and bequeathed what he had written to his son Shem before his death (Jubilees 10:13–14). Yet as we saw in Section 5.4, medieval Muslim scholars such as Ibn Barajjan counted the "scrolls of Noah" among the ancient "scrolls ennobled by the exalted revelation." Other authors in this Element likewise mentioned a book of Noah, though with less enthusiasm. The fourth-century North African bishop Augustine, for instance, listed the writings of Noah among the sacred books not admitted to the canon because they were too ancient to maintain a reliable textual tradition. As he elaborated, "the writings of these men could not be held as authoritative . . . on account of their too great antiquity, which made it seem needful to regard them with suspicion" (City of God 18.38, Latin Dombart and Kalb 2013, 313; English Dods 1881, 264). Others such as the thirteenth-century German rabbi Shimon b. Tzadok, record in some detail how a book of Noah was coauthored when "an angel came and took one of Noah's sons and brought him to the Garden of Eden and taught him all the remedies in the world. And they wrote those remedies in a book" (Tashbetz Qatan 445.1 English Scharbach 116). In other instances, Noah is described as transmitting or studying primordial books rather than writing them. The tenth-century Aramaic Samaritan chronicle the Book of Asatir relates, for instance, that "Noah sat in Adam's place after Adam's death. In the seventh year he learned three books of the covenant: the Book of the Signs, the Book of the Constellations and the Book of the Wars" (Aramaic Gaster 1927, 11, English Stone 24). The thirteenth-century work of Jewish mysticism the Zohar likewise records:

> When Noah was born he saw the deeds of human beings, sinning in the presence of the blessed Holy One, so he hid himself away, engaging in devotion to his Lord, so as not to follow in their paths. If you ask, "In what did he engage?" – the Book of Adam and the Book of Enoch, engaging in them to worship his Lord" (Zohar Bereishit 1:58b, Aramaic Bar Ilan 2023, English Matt 2004, 1.333)

While the ninth-century Muslim chronicler Abū Jaʿfar Muḥammad ibn Jarīr ibn Yazīd al-Ṭabarī tells a similar tale but depicts Noah desperately trying to teach the generation of the flood from the scrolls he had inherited from Adam and Enoch (Idris):

> God sent Noah to them to make them afraid of His awesome power and to warn them of His assault. Noah was to call upon them to repent, to return to the truth, and to act in accordance with the commands given by God to his messengers and revealed by him in the scrolls of Adam, Seth, and Enoch. (Arabic de Goeje 1897,185; English Rosenthal 1989, 377).

By the eighteenth century, the German scholar Simon Friedriche Rues could quote (with some disgust) a wide variety of such tales told by generations of Christian authors about the "writings of Enoch and Noah" and other primordial books that had survived the flood (German Rues 1748, 9, English original). Often with no obvious genealogical connections to link them, Jewish, Christian, and Muslim scholars spanning centuries and continents nevertheless came to accept the basic outlines of a shared bibliomythology about the scriptural Noah with no obvious scriptural basis.

More striking still, Jewish, Christian, and Muslim authors proceeded to produce and exchange with one another new works that claimed to be these secret writings possessed by Noah. Although only a handful of these novel apocryphal works have survived, they were not rare. The eighth-century Yemenite scholar Wahb ibn Munabbih claimed to have read ninety-three of these sorts of primordial wisdom books in his lifetime (Kohlberg 2020, 328). One Noah book that might conceivably have been counted among his library was the late antique Hebrew *Book of Secret*. This mystical work describing the heavens, angels, and the magical praxis needed to navigate the upper world survives in many Hebrew versions. But each version begins with a preface ascribing the book to Noah:

> This is a book, from the Books of Mysteries, which was given to Noah, the son of Lamech . . . .by Raziel the angel in the year when he came into the ark [but] before his entrance. And [Noah] inscribed it upon a sapphire stone very distinctly. And he learned from it how to do wondrous deeds, and [he learned] secrets of knowledge, and categories of understanding and thoughts of humility and concepts of counsel, [how] to master the investigations of the strata of the heavens, to go about in all that is in their seven abodes. (Hebrew Margaliot 1966, 58; English Morgan 2022, 17).

In the *Book of Secrets*, the notion that the scriptural Noah possessed a book of otherworldly knowledge is given a literary body. In this late antique book, any reader might (supposedly) peruse the cosmological secrets that Noah received for himself.

The *Book of Secrets* was eventually adapted into Arabic compositions that included both translated excerpts of the original text and novel additions.

Versions of the work circulated in both Christian and Muslim circles for centuries (Fodor 2006). Despite the composite nature of their editions, the owners of these Arabic texts appear to have taken the work's Noahic provenance seriously. In one dramatic cross-cultural tale from 1672, a Dominican friar named Johann Michael Wansleben travelling in Muslim Egypt acquired an Arabic copy of a book that claimed it had been preserved by Noah in the Ark. When Wansleben's own ship to Turkey hit dangerously stormy weather, the friar began to have second thoughts about his acquisition. As he writes:

> When I reflected on the misfortunes that were continually occurring to us, I became persuaded that they must be a divine castigation for some grand crime or sin that someone in our company had committed. And when I was thinking that night (which I thought was the last of my life) about my own deeds, nothing gave me scruples except the possession of an Arabic manuscript that I had with me – the most famous magical text that I could find in Egypt – which was called Sefer Adam, or the Book of Adam. It was so called because, according to its preface, the magic contained in this book was inspired in Adam by God via the angels and delivered to Noah when he entered the ark. And after the flood was preserved, according to the tradition, until this very day. Believing that I had committed a grave sin by having such a book with me, and perhaps even worse that I was carrying it to Christendom, where it might easily have come into the hands of people who would have made evil use of it, and believing that I would be doing a work acceptable to God if I threw it into the sea, to satisfy my scrupulous conscience, I threw it that very night into the sea (Italian Hamilton 407, English original).

Wansleben would ultimately regret his rashness when he could not find another copy of the manuscript. But at least in a moment of stress, the German scholar believed that he was endangering both his shipmates and his compatriots back home by transporting a powerful book of biblical magic from a Muslim country to Christian lands, where its power might be more successfully unlocked by a biblically knowledgeable but unscrupulous reader.

Both Christian and Muslim manuscripts that included Arabic translations of the *Book of Secrets* did indeed preface the work with an account similar to that described by Wansleben. One Arabic edition apparently prepared by a Coptic Christian, for instance, begins "In the Name of the Father, the Son, the Holy Spirit, One God. Amen. With the help of God and with good fortune [granted] by Him we start to copy Sifr Adam (The Book of Adam) which God, the Holy King revealed to him" (Fodor 2006 Arabic 413 English 415). Adam "asked with its help and he was proud of it in everything he did" and so likewise Noah used this miraculous book to build the Ark (Fodor 2006 Arabic 413 English 415). Meanwhile, a modern Arabic adaptation of the Book of Secrets transcribed by a Muslim copyist prefaced the work with the declaration:

It was copied from the original by Umar Lutfi the telegrapher, who relies on his God (may he be exalted.) The copy was completed on Monday, 27 Ramadan 1334, 9 August 1915 . . . (Zsom, Arabic 186 and English 184)

In the name of God, the only Creator, Living and Provider. This is the Book of Adam that God, the Omnipotent and Holy King, revealed to him. The angel (peace be upon him) accompanied him. It contains hidden knowledge, the ways of understanding and humble contemplations. [From this book] you can obtain absolute knowledge of the celestial spheres, you can learn everything that is in the seven heavens . . . (Zsom Arabic 186, English 188)

Noah (peace be upon him) had learned from the secrets of this book how to make the boat from teakwood, and he hid himself in it from the Flood . . . but the first thing he brought with him [into the Ark] was this holy book, in a golden box. He was learning from it all the time what would happen in each day, and he was asking God to fulfil his needs using this book during his whole life. And when he was dying, he handed it over to his son, Shem, after him. (Zsom Arabic 187 English 189).

In these accounts, the primordial book that saved Noah from the flood is indeed attributed to Adam but the salvation of Noah is featured as the best proof of the book's supernatural power.

The Book of Secrets tradition lived an equally storied bibliographic life in Europe, where came to be known as "the Book of Noah" and took on a medieval addition called the Book of Vestments that contained a Noahic provenance of its own. In a lengthy bibliographic preface, the Book of Vestments told an elaborate story of Noah's book similar to that outlined in the Arabic editions above:

Adam drew near and heard, learning to be guided by the holy book. Raziel, the angel, opened the book and read the words . . . Adam took the book. A great fire kindled upon the bank of the river. The angel rose up in flames and returned to heaven . . . Adam, the first man, understood the power was passed on to the generations coming after . . . It was kept hidden, until coming to serve Noah, son of Lamech, a most righteous and honest man, loved by the Lord . . . The Lord sent forth the holy prince, Raphael, to Noah. Raphael spoke, I have been sent forth by the word of Elohim . . . .I make known what will be and what to do, and deliver this holy book . . . .Behold, I give you this holy book to reveal all the secrets and mysteries . . . From it, learn how to make the ark . . . By understanding every word, every man and beast and living creature and bird and creeping thing and fish know of the power and great strength. Become wise by the great wisdom of the holy book . . . Noah was guided by the wisdom of the book. It was made known to his son, Shem. (Hebrew Jellinek 1967, 3.156–158, English Savedow 2000, 6–9)

In the prefatory tale excerpted here, Adam is identified as the first recipient of the secret book that follows – and other primordial scriptural figures such as

Enoch are acknowledged as recipients in their own right. But each new recipient merits and receives their own copy of this secret knowledge directly from an angel and the story of Noah's book remains the most elaborate tale in the series. In this sense, the Book of Vestments remained a Book of Noah while also accommodating and knitting together a wide variety of other bibliomythographies that had grown up around such primordial books – a lost Book of Adam, the apocryphal book of Enoch, and other vernacular accounts of extra-scriptural ancient knowledge.

This eclectic new preface would in turn allow these two Noahic works to be combined with other bibliomythographies that had come to be attached to a variety of other scriptural figures – including Adam, Enoch, Moses, and Solomon. This turn of events appears to have increased the work's reach considerably. A loose collection of works combining the *Book of Secrets* and the *Book of Vestments* with various additional materials came to circulate among both Jews and Christians in Europe as a work of angelology and practical mysticism called the *Book of Raziel*. The *Book of Raziel* appeared in Hebrew and Latin as well as contemporary European vernaculars such as English, French, German, and Czech. Many of these editions combined the book of Noah tradition with other biblical bibliomythographies to offer a wide variety of versions with different themes. A 1259 Latin courtly edition of this work heavily inflected with themes of Solomonic royal wisdom, for instance, was produced by the court of Alfonso X of Castile and survives in multiple copies (Riva 2020). Another Solomonic elaboration drew on the king's legendary power to subdue demons and generated a collection of Latin and vernacular works devoted to Solomonic magic. A third medieval Noah book known as the *Book of Healing Transmitted by Asaph the Physician* argued that the book Noah had received was the very Book of Healing that rabbinic tradition claimed the biblical king Hezekiah had hidden away (mPesachim 4:9, Scharbach 2010, 114). As the Book of Raziel tradition spread and diverged, the secrets of the book of Noah came to be used by an extraordinarily wide variety of Europeans – from political rulers to rabbis, magicians, and doctors.

The development of these different literary traditions did not represent a simple case of linear borrowing and elaboration, however, since scholars from different religious communities continued to draw on multiple versions of these Noah book traditions. The producer of the first Hebrew printing of the work in 1701, for instance, cited faulty French renderings of these materials as his impetus for furnishing a correct version of the text (Schorsch 2020, 167–169). While a version of the Book of Raziel produced in Italy includes a preface in which the author claims to have before him both a Hebrew and a Latin version of the text (Idel 2011, 207–208). Throughout

Europe, the scriptural vernacular produced by the Book of Raziel not only spread but also continued to double back on itself – crossing and recrossing linguistic and community boundaries over the centuries.

One might be tempted to dismiss the importance of these European works as religious productions because they contain secular medical materials or practical mysticism that could be categorized as magic. But medieval works billed as books of Noah were far from marginal in an era when medicine, mysticism, and supernatural aid were closely intertwined. In the *Book of Noah Transmitted by Asaph the Physician*, for instance, Noah's secret book was identified as a medical encyclopedia that included the Greek and Middle Eastern medical knowledge appended in the rest of the volume – generously interspersed with astrological diagrams and magical formulas. Yet despite both the secular and esoteric contents of this supposed Noah book, the famous rabbi Ovadiah of Bertinoro would mention this medieval production in his commentary on the Mishnah as an authentic biblical work. As he explained, "the Book of Healing is a work that teaches about shapes of the stars and talismans, that a certain shape made in a certain period and time heals from a certain illness, and this almost misled humanity into worshipping the stars, therefore [Hezekiah] hid it" (commentary on mPesachim 4:10, Scharbach 114–116). One finds similarly accepting references to the Book of Raziel tradition within other Jewish religious materials. The twelfth-century Iberian rabbi Abraham ibn Ezra, for instance, cites the "Book of Raziel" as an authoritative source in support of his view that a particular verse contains seventy-two letters because that is the number of letters in the most powerful divine name (Ibn Ezra on Exodus 14:19) – a citation that is then repeated in other rabbinic commentaries well into the sixteenth century (see, e.g., Toldot Yitzhak on Exodus 14:19). Other rabbinic works quote the Book of Raziel for its knowledge of hell (Kav HaYashar 87:1, seventeenth-century Germany) and its mystical account of creation (Gershon Henoch Leiner, Sod Yesharim, Seventh Day of Pesach 25, nineteenth-century Poland). In Christian circles, the actual contents of Raziel works were sometimes treated with suspicious but the bibliographic legends that gave birth to them were accepted. In various learned sermons, for instance, the fifteenth-century German cardinal Nicolas of Cusa quotes the Book of Raziel and some of its offshoots together with the works Rabbi Abraham ibn Ezra and Maimonides as examples of Jewish esoteric literature but opines:

> And in those books, which are said to have been written by Adam and his just son Abel, and in a certain book, which is ascribed to Salomon and is called Sefer Raziel (Book of Raziel), it can be found, how the ancients believed that

in this name and in the other uncountable divine names all wisdom of the
highest and of the lowest world is contained. But today the books are
destroyed because they are written in unintelligible languages, and they are
justly scorned and damned. (Latin and English Hasselhoff 2015, 31).

For Nicolas of Cusa, the poorly transmitted and corrupted texts of extant
apocryphal books attributed to ancient scriptural figures were not so much
a source of reliable practical knowledge as a witness to authorial activities of
ancient biblical figures. From an anonymous late antique Jewish author to
a twentieth-century Muslim telegraph operator, Jews, Christians and Muslims
earnestly shared, adapted, expanded, and sought supernatural aid from apocryphal books that they believed captured the divine secrets that allowed the
scriptural Noah to survive the Flood.

In literary traditions like the apocryphal book of Noah, Jews, Christians and
Muslims generated shared mythologies about scriptural figures that ventured
well beyond the stories recorded in scriptural texts. Indeed, the Jews, Christians,
and Muslims who authored, adapted, and circulated such apocryphal books
continuously generated new shared texts in a scriptural idiom. These novel texts
in turn were transmitted in Abrahamic communities across continents and
centuries until the new scriptural motifs they generated were folded back into
the traditional discourses of different communities. We sometimes imagine
Jews, Christians, and Muslims interact because of their rivalry over the correct
interpretation of ancient scripture. But we also see many examples in which
Jewish, Christian, and Muslim scholars indirectly collaborated to create new
forms of scriptural common sense beyond the bounds of existing scripture.

6 Concluding Thoughts: Moving from an Affective History to a History of Common Sense

The study of Jewish, Christian, and Muslim relations is often framed as an
affective history. That is, contemporary scholarship frequently characterizes
historical relations between Abrahamic communities in emotional terms and
evaluates intercommunal interactions based on the affection or antipathy
expressed by religious authorities toward other Abrahamic communities.
These are important questions. How a society treats its religious minorities
often has dramatic and lasting historical implications.

This Element argues, however, that the attitudes of religious practitioners
toward one another do not determine whether and to what extent two religious
communities become entangled. In the historical examples explored in this
Element, even Abrahamic communities that were ostensibly at odds with one
another often developed shared scriptural vernaculars that influenced the

religious imaginations of all players. Over the course of centuries, Jews, Christians, and Muslims from across the globe have repeatedly written other Abrahamic communities into their own sacred histories, prayed together, studied together, rebelled against religious authorities together, and coauthored a rich library of new scriptural vernaculars.

References

Abdul-Rahman, M. S. (2009) *Tafsir Ibn Kathir Juz'14: Al-Hijr 1 to An-Nahl 128*. London: MSA.

Abgaryan, G. A. (1979) *Patmut'iwn Sebeosi*. Erevan: Haykakan SSH Gitutynneri Akademiayi Hratarakcutyun.

Adang, C. (1996) *Muslim Writers on Judaism and the Hebrew Bible: From Ibn Rabban to Ibn Hazm* (Vol. 22). Leiden: Brill.

Adler, N. trans. and ed. (2004) *Jewish Travelers*. London: Routledge.

Agnew, J. (1994) The Territorial Trap: The Geographical Assumptions of International Relations Theory. *Review of International Political Economy* 1.1, pp. 53–80.

Albera, D. (2019) Ritual Mixing and Interrituality at Marian Shrines. In *Interreligious Relations and the Negotiation of Ritual Boundaries: Explorations in Interrituality*, ed. Marianne Moyaert. Cham: Springer, pp. 137–154.

Ali, S. (2010) Early Islam – – Monotheism or Henotheism? A View from the Court in Muhsin al-Musawi. In *Arabic Literary Thresholds*, ed. Muḥsin Jasim Mūsawī. Tuebingen: Mohr Siebeck, pp. 14–37.

Anidjar, G. (2009) The Idea of an Anthropology of Christianity. *Interventions* 11.3, pp. 367–393.

Arafat, S. ed. (2005) *Tafsīr al-Qur'ān al-'azīm*. Jeddah: Dar al-Hada.

Asad, T. (1986) The Idea of an Anthropology of Islam (Georgetown University Occasional Papers Series), https://books.google.com/books/about/The_Idea_of_an_Anthropology_of_Islam.html?id=uXoMRAAACAAJ.

Bakhos, C. (2014) *The Family of Abraham: Jewish, Christian, and Muslim Interpretations*. Cambridge, MA: Harvard University Press.

Bakhos, C. (2019) What Is in a Name? The Implications of "Abrahamic" for Jewish, Christian, and Muslim Relations. In *Jewish-Muslim Relations*, Wiener Beiträge zur Islamforschung, eds. Ednan Aslan and Margaret Rausch. Wiesbaden: Springer VS, pp. 3–16.

Bar-Ilan University. (2023) *The Responsa Project*. Ramat Gan: Bar-Ilan University.

Bass, S. (1806) *Sefer Sifte Yeshenim*. Zolkiew: Rabin.

Baumgarten, A. and Rustow, M. (2011) Judaism and Tradition: Continuity, Change, and Innovation. In *Jewish Studies at the Crossroads of Anthropology and History: Authority, Diaspora, Tradition*, ed. Ra'anan Boustan, Oren Kosansky, and Marina Rustow. Philadelphia: University of Pennsylvania Press, pp. 207–237.

Baumgarten, E. (2022) *Biblical Women and Jewish Daily Life in the Middle Ages*. Philadelphia: University of Pennsylvania Press.

Boewering, G. and Casewit, Y. (2016) *A Quran Commentary by Ibn Barrajan of Seville*. Leiden: Brill.

Boulding, M. trans. (2001) *Exposition of Psalms 51–72*. New York: New City Press.

Bousek, D. (2018) And the Ishmaelites Honour the Site: Images of Encounters between Jews and Muslims at Jewish Sacred Places in Medieval Hebrew Travelogues. *Archiv Orientalni* 86, pp. 23–51.

Boustan, R. and Sanzo, J. (2017) Christian Magicians, Jewish Magical Idioms, and the Shared Magical Culture of Late Antiquity. *The Harvard Theological Review* 110.2, pp. 217–240.

Brann, R. (2012) *Power in the Portrayal: Representations of Jews and Muslims in Eleventh-and Twelfth-Century Islamic Spain*. Princeton: Princeton University Press.

van Boxel, P., Macfarlane, K., and Weinberg, J. (2022) The Mishnah between Jews and Christians in Early Modern Europe. In *The Mishnaic Moment: Jewish Law among Jews and Christians in Early Modern Europe*, ed. Piet van Boxel, Kirsten Macfarlane, and Joanna Weinberg. Oxford: Oxford University Press, pp. 2–43.

Butts, A. (2021) Timothy I, Letter 47. In *Eastern Christianity: A Reader*, ed. J. Edward Walters. Grand Rapids: Eerdmans, pp. 123–128

Casewit, Y. (2016) A Muslim Scholar of the Bible: Prooftexts from Genesis and Matthew in the Qur'an Commentary of Ibn Barrajān of Seville (d. 536/1141). *Journal of Qur'anic Studies* 18.1, pp. 1–48.

Chavel, C. B. (1999) *Commentary on the Torah: Bereshit-Genesis*. New York: Shilo.

Chittick, W. C. (1989) *The Sufi Path of Knowledge: Ibn Al-'he Su's Metaphysics of Imagination*. Albany: State University of New York Press.

Chittick, W. C. (1994) *Imaginal Worlds: Ibn al-'Arabī and the Problem of Religious Diversity*. Albany: State University of New York Press.

Cohen, A. (1969) *The Myth of Judeo-Christian Tradition*. New York: Harper & Row.

Cohen, M. R. and Somekh, S. (1990) In the Court of Ya'qūb Ibn Killis: A Fragment from the Cairo Genizah. *The Jewish Quarterly Review* 80.3/4, pp. 283–314.

Corrigan, J., Denny, F., Jaffee, M. S., and Eire, C. (1998) *Jews, Christians, Muslims: A Comparative Introduction to Monotheistic Religions*. New York: Routledge.

Cuffel, A. (2003) "Henceforward All Generations Will Call Me Blessed": Medieval Christian Tales of Non-Christian Marian Veneration. *Mediterranean Studies* 12, pp. 37–60.

Dana, N. (1989) *Sefer ha-maspik le'ovdey ha-shem = Kitāb kifāyat al-'ābidīnI*. Ramat Gan: Bar Ilan University Press.

Dash-Moore, D. (2022) *Vernacular Religion: Collected Essays of Leonard Norman Primiano*. New York: New York University Press.

Decter, J. P. (2006) The Rendering of Qur'anic Quotations in Hebrew Translations of Islamic Texts. *The Jewish Quarterly Review* 96.3, pp. 336–58.

Dods, M. (1872) *The Works of Aurelius Augustine: A New Translation* (Vol. 6). Edinburgh: T. & T. Clark.

Dods, M. (1881) *The Works of Aurelius Augustine: The City of God* (Vol. 2). Edinburgh: T. & T. Clark.

Dombart, B. and Kalb, A. (1993) *Sancti Aurelii Augustini episcopi de civitate dei libri XXII*. Berlin: B. G. Teubner.

Dubovik, Y. (2018) 'Oil Which Shall Not Quit My Head': Jewish Christian Interaction in Eleventh-Century Baghdad *Entangled Religions* 6, pp. 95–123.

Dury, J. (1649) *A Seasonable Discourse*. London: R. Woodnothe (available through Early English Books Online).

Eisenstein, J. D. ed. (1926) *Ozar Massaoth: A Collection of Itineraries by Jewish Travelers to Palestine, Syria, Egypt and Other Countries; with Maps, Notes and Index*. New York: Eisenstein.

Erlewine, R. (2010) *Monotheism and Tolerance: Recovering a Religion of Reason*. Bloomington: Indiana University Press.

Fenton, P. (1982) A Jewish Sufi on the Influence of Music. *Yuval* 4, pp. 124–130.

Fenton, P. (1995) *The Treatise of the Pool= Al-Maqāla al-ḥawḍiyya*. London: Octagon Press.

Flood, G. (2020) *Hindu Monotheism (Elements in Religion and Monotheism)*. Cambridge: Cambridge University Press.

Fodor, A. (2006) An Arabic Version of Sefer Ha-Razim. *Jewish Studies Quarterly* 13.4, pp. 412–427.

Fredriksen, P. (2010) *Augustine and the Jews: A Christian Defense of Jews and Judaism*. New Haven: Yale University Press.

Fredriksen, P. (2022) Philo, Herod, Paul, and the Many Gods of Ancient Jewish "Monotheism." *Harvard Theological Review* 115.1, pp. 23–45.

Gaster, M. (1927) *The Asatir: The Samaritan Book of the "Secrets of Moses."* London: Royal Asiatic Society.

de Goeje, Michael Jan ed. (1897) *Annales quos scripsit / Abu Djafar Mohammed ibn Djarir al-Tabari*. Leiden: Brill.

Goitein, S. D. (1953) A Jewish Addict to Sufism: In the Time of the Nagid David II Maimonides. *The Jewish Quarterly Review* 44.1, pp. 37–49.

Goldstein, M. (2023) A Judeo-Arabic Parody of the Life of Jesus: The Toledot Yeshu Helene Narrative. In *A Judeo-Arabic Parody of the Life of Jesus: The Toledot Yeshu Helene Narrative*. Tuebingen: Mohr Siebeck.

Gregg, R. C. (2015) *Shared Stories, Rival Tellings: Early Encounters of Jews, Christians, and Muslims*. Oxford: Oxford University Press.

Griffith, S. (1999) The Monk in the Emir's Majlis: Reflections on a Popular Genre of Christan Literary Apologetics in Arabic in the Early Islamic Period. In *The Majlis: Interreligious Encounters in Medieval Islam*, ed. Hava Lazarus-Yafeh. Wiesbaden: Otto Harrassowitz Verlag, pp. 13–65.

Hamilton, A. ed. (2018) *Johann Michael Wansleben's Travels in the Levant, 1671–1674: An Annotated Edition of His Italian Report*. Leiden: Brill.

Hammon, A. G. (1865) *Patrologiae Cursus Completus: Series Latina* (Vol. 33). Paris: Garnier Brothers.

Harkins, P. (1979) *Discourses against Judaizing Christians: The Fathers of the Church Series* (Vol. 68). Washington, DC: Catholic University of America Press.

Harvey, P. (2019) *Buddhism and Monotheism*. Cambridge: Cambridge University Press.

Hasselhoff, G. K. (2015) The Image of Judaism in Nicholas of Cusa's Writings. *Medievalia et Humanistica* 40, pp. 25–36.

Heimgartner, M. (2012) *Die Briefe 42–58 des Ostsyrischen Patriarchen Timotheos*. Leuven: Peeters.

Hofer, N. (2014) Scriptural Substitutions and Anonymous Citations: Judaization as Rhetorical Strategy in a Jewish Sufi Text. *Numen* 61.4, pp. 364–395.

Hosni, F. ed. (2016) Tanbīh al-afhām ilā tadabbur al-kitāb al-hakīm wa-tacarruf al-āyāt wa'l-naba 3 al- cazīm, al-macrūf bi-Tafsīr Ibn Barrajan Amman: Dār al-Nur al-Mubin.

Hughes, A. (2013) *Abrahamic Religions: On the Uses and Abuses of History*. Oxford: Oxford University Press.

Hussey, R. ed. (1860) *Volume 1 of Sozomeni ecclesiastica historia: Greek Text with Latin Translation*. Oxonii: E typographeo Academico.

Idel, M. (2011) *Kabbalah in Italy, 1280–1510: A Survey*. New Haven: Yale University Press.

Ilan, T. (2013) Jesus and Joshua ben Perahiah. *Journal for the Study of Judaism* 52.3, pp. 985–995.

Ilan, Z. (1997) *Ḳivre tsadiḳim be-Erets Yiśra'el*. Jerusalem: Kanah.

Jaffee, M. (2001) One God, One Revelation, One People: On the Symbolic Structure of Elective Monotheism. *Journal of the American Academy of Religion* 69.4, pp. 753–776.

Jellinek, A. (1967) *Bet ha-Midrasch*. Jerusalem: Wachsmann Books.

Jessey, H. (1656) *A Narrative of the Late Roceeds at White-Hall Concerning the Jews*. London: Chapman.

Kohlberg, E. (2020) *In Praise of the Few: Studies in Shi'i Thought and History*. Leiden: Brill.

Kramer, J. (1986) *Humanism in the Renaissance of Islam*. Leiden: Brill.

Kraemer, J. (1992) The Andalusian Mystic Ibn Hūd and the Conversion of the Jews *Israel Oriental Studies* 12, pp. 59–73.

Kugel, J. L. (1999) *The Bible as It Was*. Cambridge, MA: Harvard University Press.

Letts, M. ed. (2017) *The Pilgrimage of Arnold von Harff, Knight, from Cologne: Through Italy, Syria, Egypt, Arabia, Ethiopia, Nubia, Palestine, Turkey, France and Spain, Which He Accomplished in the Years 1496–1499*. Milton Park: Taylor & Francis.

Levenson, J. (2012) *Inheriting Abraham: The Legacy of the Patriarch in Judaism, Christianity, and Islam*. Princeton: Princeton University Press.

Levi Strauss, C. (1987) *Introduction to the Work of Marcel Mauss* trans. Felicity Baker. London: Routledge.

Levine, D. (1908) *The Bustan al-Ukul by Nathanel ibn al-Fayyumi*. New York City, NY: Columbia University.

Le Strange, G. (1975) *Palestine under the Moslems: A Description of Syria and the Holy Land from A.D. 650 to 1500 Translated from the Works of the Medieval Arab Geographers*. New York: AMS Press.

Limor, O. (2007) Sharing Sacred Space: Holy Places in Jerusalem between Christianity, Judaism and Islam. In *In laudem Hierosolymitani: Studies in Crusades and Medieval Culture in Honour of Benjamin Z. Kedar*, ed. Ronnie Ellenblum and Iris Shagrir. Milton Park: Routledge, pp. 219–231.

Lobel, D. (2013) *A Sufi-Jewish Dialogue: Philosophy and Mysticism in Bahya ibn Paquda's" Duties of the Heart."* Philadelphia: University of Pennsylvania Press.

MacDonald, N. (2012) *Deuteronomy and the Meaning of "Monotheism."* Tuebingen: Mohr Siebeck.

Margaliot, M. (1966) *Sefer Ha-Razim*. Tel Aviv: Yediot Ahronot.

Marx, A. (1921) An Aramaic Fragment of the Wisdom of Solomon. *Journal of Biblical Literature* 40, pp. 57–69.

Matt, D. C. (2004) *The Zohar: Pritzker Edition*. Redwood City: Stanford University Press.

Mettmann, W. (1994) *Mostrador de Justicia*. Opladen: Westdeutscher Verlag.

Migne, J. P. (1864) *Patrologiae Cursus Completus: Latin Series* (Vol. 35). Paris: Garnier Brothers.

Migne, J. P. ed. (1886) *Patrologiae Cursus Completus: Latin Series* (Vol. 42). Paris: Garnier Brothers.

Migne, J. P. ed. (1891) *Patrologia Graeca* (Vol. 48). Paris: Garnier Brothers.

Miller, N. A. (2023) Reading across Confessional Lines in Ayyubid Egypt: A Judaeo-Arabic Geniza Fragment with Three New Poems by Ibn al-Kīzānī (d. 562/1166). *Bulletin of the School of Oriental and African Studies* 86, pp. 1–28.

Mingana, A. (2009) *The Apology of Timothy the Patriarch before the Caliph Mahdi: Woodbrooke Studies 2*. Piscataway: Gorgias Press.

Mitchell, S. and Van Nuffelen, P. eds. (2010) *One God: Pagan Monotheism in the Roman Empire*. Cambridge: Cambridge University Press.

Morgan, M. (2022) *Sepher Ha-Razim: The Book of Mysteries*. Atlanta: Society of Biblical Literature Press.

Nemoy, L. (1930) Al-Qirqisani's Account of the Jewish Sects. *Hebrew Union College Annual* 7, pp. 317–397.

Nemoy, L. (1939) *KitÆab al-anwÆar wal-marÆaqib: Code of Karaite law* (Vol. 1). New York: The Alexander Kohut Memorial Foundation.

Neusner, J. trans. (1991) *Talmud of the Land of Israel: Shabbat*. Chicago: University of Chicago Press.

Nicoll, A. (1816) Account of a Disputation between a Christian Monk and Three Learned Mohammedans, on the Subject of Religion. *Edinburgh Annual Register* 9, pp. 405–442.

Nutzman, M. (2022) *Contested Cures: Identity and Ritual Healing in Roman and Late Antique Palestine*. Edinburgh: Edinburgh University Press.

Penn, M. (2008) John and the Emir: A New Introduction, Edition and Translation. *Le Muséon* 121.1, pp. 65–91.

Perlmann, M. (1964) Samau'al al-Maghribī Ifḥām Al-Yahūd: Silencing the Jews. *Proceedings of the American Academy of Jewish Research* 32, pp. 1–234.

Popkin, R. H. and Katz, D. S. (1988) The Prefaces by Menasseh ben Israel and Jacob Judah Leon Templo to the Vocalized Mishnah (1646). In *Jewish-Christian Relations in the Seventeenth Century: Studies and Documents*, ed. Johannes van den Berg and Ernestine van der Wall. Dordrecht: Kluwer Academic Press, pp. 151–153.

Primiano, L. (1995) Vernacular Religion and the Search for Method in Religious Folklife. *Western Folklore* 54.1, pp. 37–56.

Pulcini, T. (1998) *Exegesis as Polemical Discourse: Ibn Ḥazm on Jewish and Christian Scriptures*. Oxford: Oxford University Press.

Reeves, J. C. (2005) *Trajectories in Near Eastern Apocalyptic: A Postrabbinic Jewish Apocalypse Reader*. Atlanta: Society of Biblical Literature.

Reiner, E. (1998), From Joshua to Jesus: The Transformation of a Biblical Story to a Local Myth (A Chapter in the Religious Life of the Galilean Jew). In *Sharing the Sacred: Religious Contacts and Conflicts in the Holy Land: 1st–15th Centuries CE*, ed. Aryeh Kofsky and Guy G. Stroumsa. Jerusalem: Yad Yitzhak Ben Tvi, pp. 233–271.

Riva, F. (2020) "Est Iste Liber Maximi Secreti": Alfonso X's Liber Razielis and the Secrets of Kingship. *Neophilologus* 104.4, pp. 485–502.

Roey, A. (1949) Une apologie syriaque attribuee a Elie de Nisibe *Le Museon* 59, pp. 383–391.

Rosenblatt, S. (1938) *The High Ways to Perfection of Abraham Maimonides Volume II*. Baltimore: Johns Hopkins Press.

Rosenthal, F. (1989) *The History of al-Tabari Vol. 1: General Introduction and from the Creation to the Flood*. Albany: State University of New York Press.

Rues, S. F. (1748) *Beweis, daß die Zeitrechnung der ersten Welt aus dem ebräischen Texte heiliger Schrift müsse genommen warden*. Tuebingen: Vierling.

Russ-Fishbane, E. (2015) *Judaism, Sufism, and the Pietists of Medieval Egypt: A Study of Abraham Maimonides and His Times*. Oxford: Oxford University Press.

Saleh, W. (2008a) *In Defense of the Bible: A Critical Edition and an Introduction to al-Biqāʿī's Bible Treatise*. Leiden: Brill.

Saleh, W. (2008b) A Fifteenth-Century Muslim Hebraist: Al-Biqāʿī and His Defense of Using the Bible to Interpret the Qurʾān. *Speculum* 83.3, pp. 629–654.

Satlow, M. (2006) Defining Judaism: Accounting for "Religions" in the Study of Religion. *Journal of the American Academy of Religion* 74.4, pp. 837–860.

Savedow, S. ed. (2000) *Sepher Rezial Hemelach: The Book of the Angel Rezial*. Boston: Weiser Books.

Schaefer, P. (2020) *Two Gods in Heaven: Jewish Concepts of God in Antiquity*. Princeton: Princeton University Press.

Scharbach, R. (June, 2010) The (Re)birth of a Book: 'Noachic' Writing in Medieval and Renaissance Europe. In *Noah and his Book(s)*, eds. Michael E. Stone, Aryeh Amichay, and Vered Hillel. Atlanta: Society of Biblical Literature Early Judaism and Its Literature Series, pp. 113–133.

Schorsch, J. (2020) Kabbalah and Cosmopolitanism in Early Modern Amsterdam: The Sephardic and Ashkenazic Producers of Sefer Raziel ha-Malakh (1701). In *Sephardim and Ashkenazim: Jewish-Jewish Encounters in History and Literature*, ed. Sina Rauschenbach. Berlin: Walter de Gruyter, pp. 155–182.

Schremer, A. (2010) *Brothers Estranged: Heresy, Christianity, and Jewish Identity in Late Antiquity.* Oxford: Oxford University Press.

Sclar, D. (2022) Cultivating Education and Piety: Menasseh ben Israel, Lay Readership, and the Printing of the Mishnah in the Seventeenth Century. In *The Mishnaic Moment: Jewish Law among Jews and Christians in Early Modern Europe*, ed. Piet van Boxel, Kirsten Macfarlane, and Joanna Weinberg. Oxford: Oxford University Press, pp. 278–298.

Shoemaker, S. (2021) *A Prophet Has Appeared: The Rise of Islam through Christian and Jewish Eyes, A Sourcebook.* Berkeley: University of California Press.

Spector, S. (2006) Forget Assimilation: Introducing Subjectivity to Jewish-German History. *Jewish History* 20.3/4, pp. 349–361.

Stampfer, Z. (2020) The Genizah within the Genizah: Muslim Works Incorporated into Judeo-Arabic Manuscripts in the Cairo Geniza. *Intellectual History of the Islamicate World* 8, pp. 265–283.

Stroumsa, G. (2015) *The Making of the Abrahamic Religions in Late Antiquity.* Oxford: Oxford University Press.

Stroumsa, G. (2021) *The Idea of Semitic Monotheism: The Rise and Fall of a Scholarly Myth.* Oxford: Oxford University Press.

Stroumsa, S. (1999) Ibn al-Rawandi's su' adab al-mujadala: The Role of Bad Manners in Medieval Disputation. In *The Majlis: Interreligious Encounters in Medieval Islam*, ed. Hava Lazarus-Yafeh. Leipzig: Otto Harrassowitz Verlag, pp. 66–83.

Stroumsa, S. (2006) *Maimonides and His World: Portrait of a Mediterranean Thinkers.* Princeton: Princeton University Press.

Stroumsa, S. (2019) *Andalus and Sefarad: On Philosophy and Its History in Islamic Spain.* Princeton: Princeton University Press.

Szpiech, R. (2012) *Conversion and Narrative: Reading and Religious Authority in Medieval Polemic.* Philadelphia: University of Pennsylvania Press.

Szpiech, R. (2022) "Right Time, Wrong Place? Navigating the 'Territorial Trap' in the Study of Medieval Religion" Plenary lecture delivered at the Leeds International Medieval Congress, 2022. University of Leeds. July 04, 2022. Available to the public at: https://youtu.be/0H8y1iMxXR8.

Teske, R. ed. and trans. (2007) *Answer to Faustus, a Manichaean (Contra Faustum Manichaeum).* New York: New City Press.

Touger, E. (1993) *Mishneh Torah*. New York: Moznaim.

Van Der Wall, E. G. (1988) "Without Partialitie towards All Men": John Durie on the Dutch Hebraist Adam Boreel. In *Jewish-Christian Relations in the Seventeenth Century: Studies and Documents*, ed. Johannes van der Berg and Ernestine van der Wall. Dordrecht: Kluwer, pp. 145–149.

Van der Wall, E. G. (1989) The Dutch Hebraist Adam Boreel and the Mishnah Project Six Unpublished Letters. *LIAS* 16, pp. 239–263.

Von Groote, E. (1860) *Die Pilgerfahrt des Ritters Arnold von Harff*. Coeln: Heberle.

Vollandt, R. (2018) Flawed Biblical Translations into Arabic and How to Correct Them: A Copt and a Jew Study Saadiah's Tafsīr in *Heirs of the Apostles*, eds. : David Bertaina, Sandra Toenies Keating, Mark N. Swanson, and Alexander Treiger. Leiden: Brill, pp. 56–92.

Wiegers, G. A. (1994) *Islamic Literature in Spanish and Aljamiado: Yça of Segovia*. Leiden: Brill.

Williams, M. H. (2008a) Lessons from Jerome's Jewish Teachers: Exegesis and Cultural Interaction in Late Antique Palestine. In *Jewish Biblical Interpretation and Cultural Exchange: Comparative Exegesis in Context*, ed. Natalie Dohrmann, pp. 66–86. Philadelphia: University of Pennsylvania Press.

Williams, M. H. (2008b). *The Monk and the Book: Jerome and the Making of Christian Scholarship*. Chicago: University of Chicago Press.

Wolf, A. M. (2014) *Juan de Segovia and the Fight for Peace: Christians and Muslims in the Fifteenth Century*. Southbend: University of Notre Dame Press.

Wollenberg, R. S. (2019) The Book That Changed: Narratives of Ezran Authorship as Late Antique Biblical Criticism. *Journal of Biblical Literature* 138.1, pp. 143–160.

Yaari, A. (1948) *Masa Meshullam mi-Volterra be 'Eretz Yisrael bi'shanat 1481*. Jerusalem: Bialik.

Yahia, O. (1968) *Futuhat al-makkiyya*. Beirut: Dar Ihya al-Turath al-Arabi.

el- Zein, A. (1977) Beyond Ideology and Theology: The Search for the Anthropology of Islam. *Annual Review of Anthropology* 6, pp. 227–254.

Zsom, D. (2015) Sufi Stories from the Cairo Genizah. *Arabist* 36, pp. 89–104.

Cambridge Elements ☰

Religion and Monotheism

Paul K. Moser
Loyola University Chicago
Paul K. Moser is Professor of Philosophy at Loyola University Chicago. He is the author of *God in Moral Experience; Paul's Gospel of Divine Self-Sacrifice; The Divine Goodness of Jesus; Divine Guidance; Understanding Religious Experience; The God Relationship; The Elusive God* (winner of national book award from the Jesuit Honor Society); *The Evidence for God; The Severity of God; Knowledge and Evidence* (all Cambridge University Press); and *Philosophy after Objectivity* (Oxford University Press); coauthor of *Theory of Knowledge* (Oxford University Press); editor of *Jesus and Philosophy* (Cambridge University Press) and *The Oxford Handbook of Epistemology* (Oxford University Press); and coeditor of *The Wisdom of the Christian Faith* (Cambridge University Press). He is the coeditor with Chad Meister of the book series *Cambridge Studies in Religion, Philosophy, and Society*.

Chad Meister
Affiliate Scholar, Ansari Institute for Global Engagement with Religion, University of Notre Dame
Chad Meister is Affiliate Scholar at the Ansari Institute for Global Engagement with Religion at the University of Notre Dame. His authored and co-authored books include *Evil: A Guide for the Perplexed* (Bloomsbury Academic, 2nd edition); *Introducing Philosophy of Religion* (Routledge); *Introducing Christian Thought* (Routledge, 2nd edition); and *Contemporary Philosophical Theology* (Routledge). He has edited or co-edited the following: *The Oxford Handbook of Religious Diversity* (Oxford University Press); *Debating Christian Theism* (Oxford University Press); with Paul Moser, *The Cambridge Companion to the Problem of Evil* (Cambridge University Press); and with Charles Taliaferro, *The History of Evil* (Routledge, in six volumes). He is the co-editor with Paul Moser of the book series *Cambridge Studies in Religion, Philosophy, and Society*.

About the Series
This Cambridge Element series publishes original concise volumes on monotheism and its significance. Monotheism has occupied inquirers since the time of the Biblical patriarch, and it continues to attract interdisciplinary academic work today. Engaging, current, and concise, the Elements benefit teachers, researched, and advanced students in religious studies, Biblical studies, theology, philosophy of religion, and related fields.

Cambridge Elements ≡

Religion and Monotheism

Elements in the Series

A full series listing is available at: www.cambridge.org/er&m

Printed in the USA
CPSIA information can be obtained
at www.ICGtesting.com
LVHW011557230824
789095LV00004B/403